The Blackbirch Visual Encyclopedia

Physical Science

BLACKBIRCH®
PRESS

THOMSON
GALE

San Diego • Detroit • New York • San Francisco • Cleveland • New Haven, Conn. • Waterville, Maine • London • Munich

CONTENTS

THOMSON
GALE

© 2002 by Blackbirch Press™. Blackbirch Press™ is an imprint of The Gale Group, Inc., a division of Thomson Learning, Inc.

Blackbirch Press™ and Thomson Learning™ are trademarks used herein under license.

For more information, contact
The Gale Group, Inc.
27500 Drake Rd.
Farmington Hills, MI 48331-3535
Or you can visit our Internet site at http://www.gale.com

Copyright © 2000 Orpheus Books Ltd. Created and produced by Nicholas Harris, Joanna Turner, and Claire Aston, Orpheus Books Ltd.

Text credit: Steve Parker, Nicholas Harris

Consultant credit: David Hawksett, researcher in planetary science, University of Lancaster

Illustration credit: Susanna Addario, Elisabetta Ferrero, Giuliano Fornari, Andrea Ricciardi di Gaudesi, Gary Hincks, Shane Marsh, Lee Montgomery, Steve Noon, Sebastian Quigley, Alessandro Rabatti, Eric Robson, Claudia Saraceni, Roger Stewart, Thomas Trojer, Mark Wilkinson, Martin Woodward, David Wright

Photographs on page 7, 11, and 37: The Illustrated London News Picture Library

LIBRARY OF CONGRESS CATALOGING-IN-PUBLICATION DATA

Harris, Nicholas, 1956-
Physical science / Nicholas Harris.
    p. cm. — (Blackbirch visual encyclopedia)
    Includes index.
    Summary: A visual encyclopedia of topics in the physical sciences, including chemistry, physics, the universe, and the solar system.
    ISBN 1-56711-521-7 (lib. bdg. : alk. paper)
    1. Physical sciences—Juvenile literature. [1. Physical sciences—Encyclopedias.] I. Series.
Q163.P5762 2003
503—dc21   2002018655

Printed in Singapore
10 9 8 7 6 5 4 3 2 1

CONTENTS

MATTER

EVERYTHING is made of matter. Every object, substance, chemical, and material is matter. This includes not only things you can see easily, like the paper of this page and the ink that forms the words and pictures. It also includes specks of dust too small to notice, houses, and cars, living things like trees and your own body, the rocks of the earth, the clouds in the sky and the invisible air around you. And not only objects and substances on the earth are made of matter. All of the planets and stars in deep space contain matter. In fact everything in the entire universe is made of matter. All matter is made of tiny building blocks called atoms (see page 6).

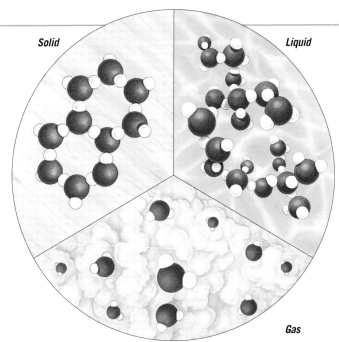

Solid Liquid

Gas

STATES OF MATTER

Matter exists in three main forms, called the states of matter. These are solid, liquid, and gas. In a solid such as ice, the molecules (atoms bonded together, see page 12) are very close together and joined in a rigid pattern. They can hardly move. So a solid object stays the same volume and does not change its shape. In a liquid such as water, the molecules are still quite close together but they are not joined to each other. They can move about, which means the whole liquid can change shape and flow, although, like the solid, it still takes up the same volume. In a gas like water vapor, the molecules can move nearer together or farther apart. So a gas can also get bigger or smaller, to fill the container it is in.

Why is a butterfly like a lump of rock whizzing through space? Both are made of atoms. The butterfly is living matter, the rock nonliving matter.

There *are* places where there is no matter. If there is no matter then there is nothing at all. The total or complete absence of matter is called a vacuum. However a total vacuum is very unusual. "Space" is named because it is supposed to be just empty space, with no matter. But even in the depths of space, a few microparticles of dust or some wispy bits of gas are floating about. These tiny bits of matter may be several feet apart, instead of crammed together like they are on Earth. But they are still present. Here on the earth, powerful vacuum pumps can suck most of the matter out of a container, but never quite all of it.

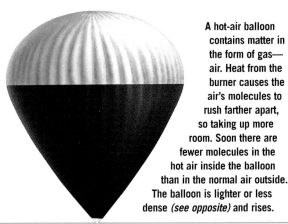

A hot-air balloon contains matter in the form of gas— air. Heat from the burner causes the air's molecules to rush farther apart, so taking up more room. Soon there are fewer molecules in the hot air inside the balloon than in the normal air outside. The balloon is lighter or less dense (see opposite) and rises.

CHANGING STATES

Matter or substance can change state from solid to liquid, or liquid to gas. This usually happens by adding heat. Matter can also change state the other way from gas to liquid or liquid to solid. This usually happens by cooling (taking away heat). A common example which is all around us is water. The world's water is always on the move and changing state in a never-ending process, the water cycle *(below)*.

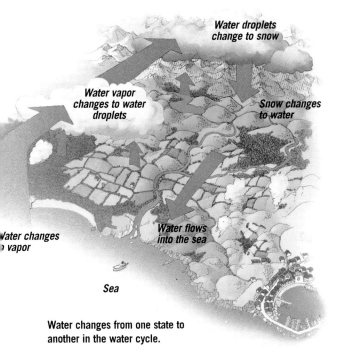

Water droplets change to snow

Water vapor changes to water droplets

Snow changes to water

Water flows into the sea

Water changes to vapor

Sea

Water changes from one state to another in the water cycle.

In the water cycle, the Sun warms the sea. The heat makes liquid water turn into a gas, invisible water vapor, which rises into the sky. It is cooler high up so water vapor changes state back into a liquid, forming tiny droplets. These are so light that they float as clouds. Wind blows the droplets over the land. Some clump together, become too heavy to float, and fall as rain. Some droplets blow even higher, up over a mountain, and become even colder. They change state again, freezing solid into snowflakes. The snow falls to the ground and melts into liquid water. With the rain, it flows into streams and rivers, and finally into the sea—and so the cycle continues.

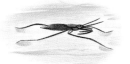

We are too big and heavy to float on liquid water. But the insect called the pond skater can do just this. Its body is very light and it slides or skates about on the surface film, which is like a tight skin stretched over the top of the water.

PROPERTIES OF MATTER

Matter has many features, or properties. One of the main properties is its state—solid, liquid, or gas. Another property is the type of atoms it is made of. Each kind of pure substance, like iron, carbon, oxygen, or sulphur, has a different kind of atom. It is known as a chemical element *(see page 6)*.

A third property of matter is density. This is the amount of matter in a certain place or volume. The more matter within a certain volume, the denser or heavier the substance or object. Dense substances like iron have lots of large atoms packed close together. Density is important because it determines whether things float or sink. If an object is less dense than water, such as a lump of wood, it floats. A lump of iron is more dense than water and so it sinks. But if the iron is made into a boat's hull its shape contains lots of air, which has a very low density and is extremely light. The overall density of the iron-plus-air is less than the density of water, and makes the boat float.

ATOMS

ALL MATTER is made of atoms. An individual atom is far too small to see, even with the most powerful microscope. But atoms joined together make up every solid object, substance, chemical, and material in the universe. A pinhead, for example, contains about one billion billion atoms.

Atoms able to move about make up liquids and gases. Atoms which are more fixed and unable to move much make up solids. Not all atoms are the same. There are about 92 different kinds of atoms that occur naturally. Scientists have made another 17 or so artificial kinds in laboratories. Each kind of atom has individual properties that distinguish it in some way from another kind. A substance made from just one kind of atom is known as a chemical element. Examples of six elements are shown below.

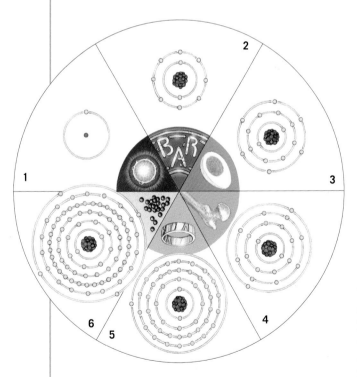

Atoms of different chemical elements have different numbers of particles. Simplest is hydrogen (1), a very light gas that makes up most of the Sun *(see pages 11, 42)*. Neon (2) is a gas used in colored lights. Egg yolks are rich in sulphur (3). Calcium (4) is needed for healthy bones. Silver (5) is a shiny valuable metal. Lead (6) has many particles and so is very heavy. It is used to make small weights or shot.

Atoms are not solid, like marbles. In fact, they are mostly empty space. But this space contains even smaller pieces of matter known as subatomic particles. There are three main kinds of subatomic particles—protons, neutrons, and electrons. The protons and neutrons are gathered together in the middle of the atom, forming its central part or nucleus. The electrons are much smaller and move quickly around the nucleus. They do not move at random, but stay in certain layers known as shells.

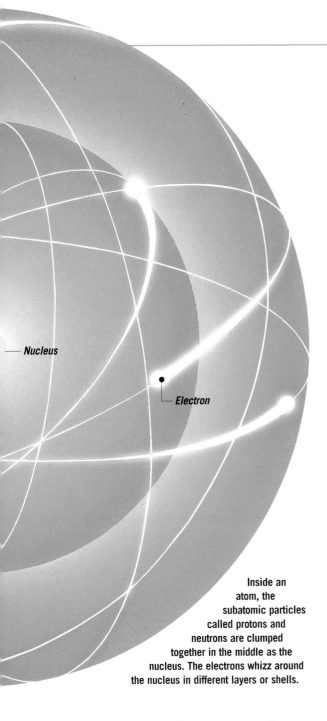

— *Nucleus*

└ *Electron*

Inside an atom, the subatomic particles called protons and neutrons are clumped together in the middle as the nucleus. The electrons whizz around the nucleus in different layers or shells.

The name "radioactivity" was invented by Polish-born scientist Marie Curie (1867-1934). She studied various rocks and minerals from the earth and gave the name to the invisible rays or particles that some of them gave off, which affected photographic paper and various electrical equipment. In particular Curie worked with the substance pitchblende, a raw material used to obtain the metal uranium. Pitchblende gave off more radioactivity than expected from uranium alone. Curie purified the substances which gave off this extra radiation and so discovered two new elements, polonium and radium.

RADIOACTIVITY

Most atoms are stable. They remain the same through time. Others are unstable— they are likely to break up. As they do so they give off some of their particles or energy in the form of rays. These particles or rays are known as radioactivity. Examples of chemical elements with radioactive atoms include uranium, plutonium, and radium. As atoms give out particles or rays they change into the atoms of simpler elements. For example, uranium changes into lead. This change is called radioactive decay. It happens at different speeds or rates for different radioactive elements. The time taken for half of a number of atoms to decay is known as the half-life of that element. Radioactivity can be dangerous since it harms living things. But under controlled conditions it is very useful in medicine and scientific research.

Elements differ in their numbers of subatomic particles. Hydrogen is the simplest because its atom has just two particles, one proton and one electron. In most atoms there are the same number of protons as electrons. This is because a proton has a tiny positive electrical charge *(see page 30)*, and an electron has the same amount of negative charge. The two sets of opposite charges balance each other out so the whole atom has no charge. This makes it stable or unlikely to break up.

How do we know the age of mummies from ancient Egypt? By measuring the tiny amounts of radioactive substances they contain. This is known as radiocarbon dating.

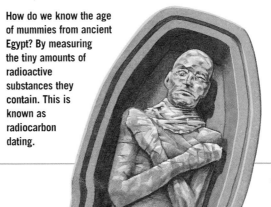

METALS

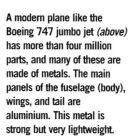

CHEMICAL ELEMENTS can be divided into several groups. The largest group, forming about three-quarters of all elements, is the metals. Metals have several features that the other elements or nonmetals lack. They carry heat and electricity very well compared to nonmetals. They are solid at normal or room temperature. They are strong, hard, and tough, and they can be polished to give a smooth, shiny surface. When they are squeezed under great pressure, they change shape or deform and become squashed, rather than splinter apart or shatter. These features are true of most metals, but not all. The metal sodium is very soft, while the metal mercury is a silvery liquid at normal temperature.

A modern plane like the Boeing 747 jumbo jet *(above)* has more than four million parts, and many of these are made of metals. The main panels of the fuselage (body), wings, and tail are aluminium. This metal is strong but very lightweight.

Not all metals stay hard and solid. Some can burn very brightly, especially in powdered form. Fireworks *(below)* contain mixtures of powdered metals such as magnesium as well as other substances to make them flare up with bright colors.

The Statue of Liberty in New York *(left)* is made of a thin shell of copper held up by a framework inside. Copper is shiny brown when clean. After a time exposed to air it develops a greenish covering of the substance copper oxide. Most cars *(below)* have bodywork made of steel plate. This is strong, easy to shape into curved panels, and relatively light. But steel is mostly iron, and iron rusts away when exposed to moisture and air. So the steel panels receive an antirust coating before they are painted.

Metals are very important in the modern world. Because of their strength and hardness they are used to make all kinds of buildings, structures, machines, and engines. The most widely-used metal in industry is iron—but not usually in its pure form. Iron is mixed with small amounts of other substances, especially carbon *(see page 10)*, to form steel. A metal mixed with other metals and substances like this is known as an alloy. There are hundreds of different kinds of alloy steels, each with slightly different amounts of carbon and other elements, and each designed to do a different task. Stainless steel is used for sinks and cutlery. Titanium and vanadium steels resist very high temperatures without melting.

In a suspension bridge, the road or railway is hung from massively thick cables made from steel that is high tensile (resists stretching).

MAKING METALS

Very rarely a lump of pure metal is found lying on the ground, such as a gold nugget. But most metals occur inside rocks. Rock especially rich in a certain metal is called a metal ore. The metal is separated from its ore by various means. Iron is obtained from ores by heating them until they melt, a process called smelting.

PRECIOUS METALS

Certain types of metals are precious or valuable. This may be because they are rare and difficult to obtain from their ores, so owning them has become a symbol of power and wealth. Some metals are prized for their beautiful colors and luster or sheen. Some are valuable because they are easy to hammer or cast into detailed, intricate shapes such as thin wires or leaves.

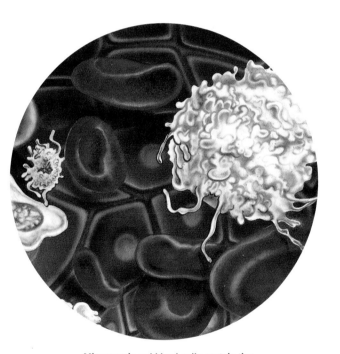

Microscopic red blood cells contain tiny particles of iron, part of the oxygen-carrying substance hemoglobin.

Two of the main precious metals are gold *(above)* and silver. People have fought wars and killed for them. These metals have become even more valuable recently because they are excellent carriers of electricity. They are used in switches, circuits, and other devices in electrical equipment. Silver is also mixed with another metal, mercury, to make tooth fillings.

Aluminium ore is known as bauxite. To separate the aluminium, it is treated with chemicals and electricity is passed through it, a process called electrolysis.

An ordinary ax would cut as well as this Viking ax, but the silver decorations show the owner's wealth and power.

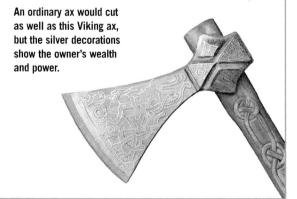

CARBON

ONE OF THE MOST important chemical elements is carbon—partly because it makes up one-fifth of the human body. It is also the main element in all living things and the sixth most common element in the universe.

Atoms of carbon can join or bond easily with each other and also with numerous other atoms *(see page 12)*. This allows carbon to be the basis of a vast variety of substances, from wood to plastics. Indeed carbon is such a common and adaptable element that it has its own branch of science, known as organic chemistry.

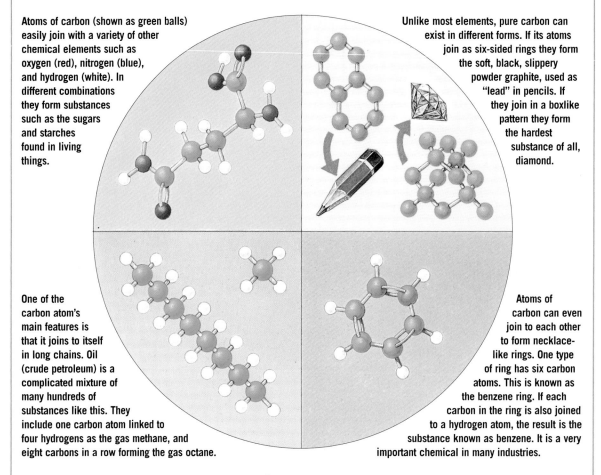

Atoms of carbon (shown as green balls) easily join with a variety of other chemical elements such as oxygen (red), nitrogen (blue), and hydrogen (white). In different combinations they form substances such as the sugars and starches found in living things.

Unlike most elements, pure carbon can exist in different forms. If its atoms join as six-sided rings they form the soft, black, slippery powder graphite, used as "lead" in pencils. If they join in a boxlike pattern they form the hardest substance of all, diamond.

One of the carbon atom's main features is that it joins to itself in long chains. Oil (crude petroleum) is a complicated mixture of many hundreds of substances like this. They include one carbon atom linked to four hydrogens as the gas methane, and eight carbons in a row forming the gas octane.

Atoms of carbon can even join to each other to form necklace-like rings. One type of ring has six carbon atoms. This is known as the benzene ring. If each carbon in the ring is also joined to a hydrogen atom, the result is the substance known as benzene. It is a very important chemical in many industries.

The structures and substances in all living things are based on carbon. This includes our own skin, hair, blood, muscles, bones, and brain, as well as the body parts of birds, fish, insects, and worms, and all the parts of plants. Even the chemicals which form our genes, known as DNA, have carbon as their main element. This is why the chemistry of carbon is often called "the chemistry of life itself."

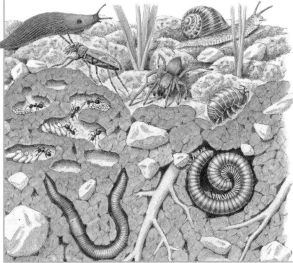

The entire living world is based on carbon. It joins with other substances to form snail shells, spiders' legs, ants' eggs, plant roots, and countless other parts.

OXYGEN

WE CANNOT see, smell, or taste oxygen. Yet it forms one-fifth of air and is vital for life. We must breathe oxygen to stay alive. So must all animals and plants.

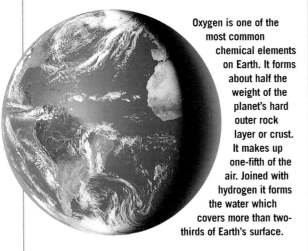

Oxygen is one of the most common chemical elements on Earth. It forms about half the weight of the planet's hard outer rock layer or crust. It makes up one-fifth of the air. Joined with hydrogen it forms the water which covers more than two-thirds of Earth's surface.

Oxygen is a vital part of chemical changes inside each microscopic living cell, which break apart food substances to obtain the energy for life. This is why oxygen is essential for all living things (except for a few specialized types of microbes).

Oxygen is also needed for burning. A substance such as coal or wood burns by splitting apart and joining with oxygen to form new substances. It quickly gives out lots of heat and often light in the process. This is known as combustion (burning).

Substances burn by joining with oxygen and giving out energy as heat and light. The welding torch burns acetylene gas.

HYDROGEN

THE MOST abundant element in the universe is hydrogen. It forms the bulk of most stars. On Earth, most hydrogen (chemical symbol·H) is joined to oxygen (O) to form water (H_2O). Hydrogen is also the simplest and lightest chemical element because each of its atoms has only two subatomic particles, one proton and one electron (see page 6).

Pure hydrogen gas is much lighter or less dense than air (see page 5). It filled the great airships of the early 20th century to keep them aloft. However, hydrogen also burns very easily. After several disasters where airships caught fire, hydrogen was no longer used. Today airships use another light gas, helium, which does not burn.

Hydrogen joins with carbon to form the substances known as hydrocarbons. Many of the fuel gases obtained from natural gas or crude oil, such as propane and butane, are hydrocarbons. Hydrogen also joins with carbon and oxygen to form carbohydrates. Starches in foods like potatoes and rice, and sugars in cane or beet, are carbohydrates.

The Sun and other stars are mostly mostly made of hydrogen. In the star's center, tremendous temperatures and pressures squash hydrogen atoms together to form atoms of the gas helium. As this happens, huge amounts of energy are released as heat and light. The energy travels up to the Sun's glowing surface and then passes through space to Earth. This is known as nuclear fusion (see page 21) because the centers, or nuclei, of the hydrogen atoms join or fuse together. Nuclear energy on Earth is obtained by splitting nuclei apart, known as nuclear fission.

MOLECULES

ATOMS make up all the objects and substances in our world. But they are rarely single atoms, alone or unattached. They are usually attached or joined to other atoms. For example, the oxygen gas that makes up one-fifth of the air does not float about as single atoms of oxygen, O. It is in the form of oxygen atoms joined together in pairs, O_2. Two or more atoms linked or joined together make a molecule. O_2 is a molecule of oxygen.

If atoms of one chemical element join or combine with atoms from other elements, this forms a compound. O_2 is a molecule of oxygen but not a compound. Two atoms of hydrogen and one of oxygen form H_2O, which is a molecule and a compound. Some compounds, like minerals in rocks, have 50 or 100 atoms in each molecule from 15 or 20 different elements. Other compounds, like certain plastics, have millions of atoms in each molecule but usually from only a few elements, mainly carbon, hydrogen, oxygen, and nitrogen. The links between atoms are called bonds. There are different types of bonds depending on the atom's structure and the conditions such as temperature and pressure.

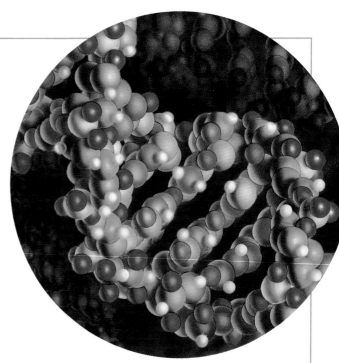

The molecule known as DNA, found in our genes, is based on a group of atoms called ribose sugar, which is repeated millions of times in a long, coiled chain.

One of the main features of the chemical element carbon is that it joins or bonds easily with many other types of atoms and also with itself *(see page 10)*. Carbon atoms can join like links in a chain to form enormously long molecules. Often the chain is made of the same groups of atoms, called subunits, which are repeated hundreds or thousands of times along its length. This type of molecule is called a polymer and the repeated subunits are monomers. Many types of plastics and artificial fibers like rayon, acrylic, and nylon are polymers. So are molecules in living things like cellulose in plants, chitin in insect body casings, and the carrier of genetic information, DNA *(see above)*.

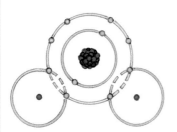

In a covalent bond one atom shares an outer electron *(see page 6)* with the next atom. Here, two hydrogen atoms are bonded covalently to one oxygen to form water, H_2O.

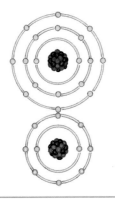

In an ionic bond an atom loses or gains electrons, which are negative. An atom that loses one becomes positive while an atom that gains one becomes negative. Atoms which are positive or negative are known as ions *(see opposite)*. Positive and negative attract and form an ionic bond. Here sodium and chlorine bond as sodium chloride, or table salt.

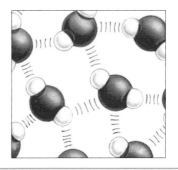

An intermolecular bond is a weak attraction between the positive part of a molecule and the negative part of its neighbor. The weak attractions between hydrogen and oxygen in water molecules are shown here.

CRYSTALS

IN MANY SOLID substances, the atoms or molecules are fixed in place but they are not positioned at random. They are arranged in an orderly or regular pattern known as a crystalline framework. The result is that the substance forms crystals. These are not irregular lumps but orderly, geometric shapes with sharp edges and flat sides at certain angles to each other. Many pure metals have a crystalline structure. So do minerals in the rocks, and sugar and salt.

Quartz

Ice

Crystals of quartz in sand grains have a triangular shape. Ice crystals form snowflakes and are six-sided.

There are seven basic shapes or systems of crystals. Simplest is the cubic shape which is like a box. Diamonds are cubic crystals. The monoclinic system is like a matchbox which has been squashed slightly flat. The calcium-rich mineral gypsum has this shape. Some natural minerals like ruby and emerald form large, shiny crystals with beautiful colors. They are cut and polished as gemstones.

Tiny crystals of minerals in many kinds of rocks fit together like miniature building blocks to form much bigger regular shapes. These hexagonal (six-sided) pillars are made of the rock basalt.

SOLUTIONS

STIR A TEASPOON of table salt into a glass of water—and the salt disappears. However, tasting the water shows the salt is still there. It has dissolved. The large grains or crystals of salt have broken down into their individual atoms. These are too small to see and float about freely among the molecules of water. The substance which dissolves, which is usually a crystalline solid, is the solute. The substance it dissolves in, usually a liquid, is the solvent. The solute in the solvent is known as a solution.

When substances dissolve, their atoms or molecules usually gain or lose electrons *(see page 6)*. For example table salt, sodium chloride (NaCl), dissolves and breaks apart into its atoms of sodium (Na) and chlorine (Cl). Sodium loses an electron and becomes positive (Na^+), while chlorine gains an electron and becomes negative (Cl^-). Atoms which are positive or negative are known as ions *(see opposite)*. Many solutes form ions.

The sea contains dissolved salt. The Dead Sea has so much that no more can dissolve: a saturated solution.

Shaking salt and sand together produces a mixture, which is different from a solution. In a mixture two or more substances intermingle but they do not dissolve and their molecules do not alter by becoming ions. Add water to the mixture and the salt dissolves. It is soluble. The sand grains do not dissolve. They are insoluble.

ACIDS AND BASES

SOME SUBSTANCES and chemicals are very reactive. This means they easily combine or join with other substances in chemical reactions to form new substances. Two types of reactive chemicals are acids and bases. Many bases dissolve in water: these are called alkalis. Strong or concentrated acids and alkalis are so reactive that they are corrosive. This means they break down and dissolve substances, including human skin, to cause severe chemical burns. Examples are the sulphuric acid in a car battery and the alkali sodium hydroxide, which is used as a drain cleaner. Strong alkalis may also be slippery or slimy, almost like thin jelly.

A weak acid usually has a sharp or sour taste, like the natural citric acid in citrus fruits such as lemons and grapefruits. A weak alkali has a bitter taste, such as the caffeine in coffee. Caffeine is an example of an alkaloid—a natural alkali found in certain plants. Many plants make alkaloids in their leaves and stems. These are poisonous so that animals avoid eating them. Some animals have bites or stings that inject poisonous acid into prey or enemies.

The fumes from vehicle exhausts, factories, and power stations contain nitrogen and sulphur chemicals. These dissolve in the drops of water in clouds to form nitric and sulphuric acids which fall as acid rain.

The human body contains a strong acid. This is hydrochloric acid, found in the stomach. It is made in the stomach lining in an inactive form, and released when food enters the stomach during a meal. The acid is very corrosive and helps to break down the nutrients in food as part of digestion. It also helps to kill any dangerous microbes (germs) that might be in the food. The stomach lining protects itself from being dissolved by its own acid by making a thick layer of slimy mucus.

A bee's sting contains a mix of poisonous substances including acidic apitoxin. The bee leaves its barb and poison sack in the skin. The sting can be treated by rubbing on a weak solution of bicarbonate of soda (baking soda), an alkali that counteracts the acid.

Acids are substances with hydrogen in their molecules. For example, sulphuric acid is H_2SO_4 and hydrochloric acid is HCl. In solution with water, the hydrogen forms a positive ion, H^+ *(see page 13).* This hydrogen ion is, in fact, a hydrogen atom without its electron—that is, it is just a proton *(see page 6).* An acid is reactive because it is always ready to give up, or donate, this proton in a chemical change, in order to rid itself of the positive charge and become neutral. Alternatively, the acid can accept an electron, which is negative, to achieve the same result. This is why acids are known as proton donors or electron receptors. An alkali does the opposite and so is a proton receptor or electron donor.

ACID OR ALKALI?

Touching or tasting an unknown liquid to find out if it is an acid or alkali is far too dangerous—even deadly. The usual way is to use an indicator. This is a substance which changes its color when added to an acid or alkali. One of the best-known indicators is litmus. It can be used as a liquid or on a dry paper strip. Normally litmus is a pink color. When it is added to an acid it turns red. Added to an alkali it becomes blue. If litmus does not change color when added to a substance then the substance is neither acid or alkali but neutral. Normal rainwater is a very weak natural acid because it contains tiny amounts of dissolved carbon dioxide, one of the gases in air, which forms carbonic acid. Acid rain from pollution is much stronger *(see opposite)*.

Like a bee, a wasp has a painful sting— also acidic, rather than alkaline as is popularly believed. The pain can be treated with a weak solution of ammonia, which is an alkali that neutralizes the acid in the sting.

In medieval times the terrible plague killed millions. The dead bodies were sprinkled with lime, a strong and corrosive base. It helped to kill the germs in the bodies and make them rot faster.

Acids and alkalis are widely used in industry. Millions of tons of sulphuric acid are produced every year, not only for vehicle batteries but for processes such as making detergents, explosives, fertilizers, and dyes for coloring. Sulphuric acid is also used in the splitting or refining of crude oil (petroleum) to make gasoline, diesel, plastics, paints, and other petroleum products.

Acids and alkalis are very important in farming and forestry. Some soils are naturally slightly acidic, others are slightly alkaline. Each type of plant grows best in a certain type of soil, acidic or neutral or alkaline. To grow a certain plant the soil can be changed using additives. Adding alkaline lime to an acidic soil makes it more neutral.

GRAVITY

THE UNIVERSE is made of matter. Matter is held together and moved by forces. One of the basic or fundamental forces is the gravitational force. Any piece of matter from a pinhead to a planet has this gravitational force. It pulls or attracts other matter. The biggest large lump of matter in our daily lives is the earth. Its gravitational force pulls us and other objects toward it, keeping our feet on the ground. Earth's gravitational force is also called gravity.

The pulling force of the Sun's gravity keeps the planets in orbit.

Gravity means that all matter, from the minute particles that make up atoms to the biggest stars, attracts each other. The nearer an object, the stronger its gravitational force on other objects. But the force becomes weaker with increasing distance. Earth is very big and very near, so for us its gravity is very strong. However, a few hundred miles above the surface its gravity is weak and objects may drift off into space.

It is said that English scientist Isaac Newton (1642–1727) had the idea for gravitational force when he saw an apple fall from a tree. Why did it fall straight down toward Earth's center? Newton suggested that the earth pulled it down by gravity. He extended this idea to all matter and into space. He proposed that the earth's gravity attracted the Moon and kept it in orbit around Earth. Newton's ideas began a new era in science.

The Moon's gravity pulls the water of Earth's oceans and makes it bulge outwards. As Earth spins this causes the rise and fall of tides.

Earth's gravity gives matter and objects what we call weight. A big book is weighty because it is being pulled downward by Earth's gravity and we have to counteract this force with our muscles when we pick up the book. However, weight varies according to the strength of gravity, and the strength of gravity depends on the amount of matter (and its density) in the two objects that attract each other. We are used to the weight of objects on Earth. The Moon has less matter than Earth, so its gravitational force is less. On the Moon the book would weigh less—about one-sixth of what it weighs on Earth. On a star consisting of vast amounts of matter the book would weigh many tons.

In space, Earth's gravity is weak. These astronauts are therefore "weightless."

Weight varies with gravitational force but mass does not. Weight is a measure of the gravitational force pulling on an object. Mass is a measure of the amount of matter in the object—the numbers and types of atoms. On Earth, the Moon, or a star, the book would weigh different amounts, but it would always have the same mass.

FORCES

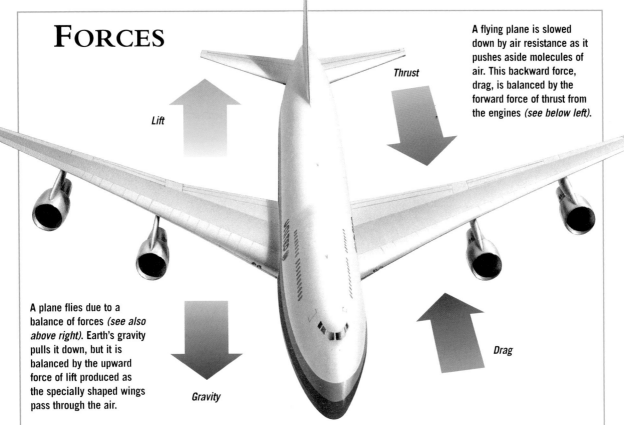

Lift

Thrust

A flying plane is slowed down by air resistance as it pushes aside molecules of air. This backward force, drag, is balanced by the forward force of thrust from the engines *(see below left)*.

A plane flies due to a balance of forces *(see also above right)*. Earth's gravity pulls it down, but it is balanced by the upward force of lift produced as the specially shaped wings pass through the air.

Gravity

Drag

A FORCE pushes or pulls. It squashes or stretches. It presses on an object or any other form of matter. It may make the object move in a certain way (motion) or change its shape (deform). One of the main forces that acts throughout the universe is the gravitational force *(see opposite)*. Another is the electromagnetic force *(see page 30)*. These two forces can act at a distance. That is, they do not have to be in contact with an object or touching it.

Physical forces act when two objects are in contact. Hammer a nail into wood, and the force of the hammer hitting the nail makes it push down into the wood's fibers. This is a force causing motion. The wood pushes back with its own resisting force. As the nail goes deeper the resisting force of the wood increases. It may eventually become equal to the force of the hammer hitting the nail. At this stage the nail stops moving. The next blow may bend the nail. This is a force causing deformation.

A lilytrotter (jacana) has wide, splayed toes which spread the force of its steps. It can easily run over floating lily leaves.

PRESSURE

The force of a hammer blow pushing a nail into wood acts over a tiny area—the nail's point. The same hammer blow might not make a blunt nail enter the wood because the force is spread out over a larger area. The amount of force for a certain area is called pressure. A sharp knife cuts because the force moving the blade is concentrated into the tiny area of the blade's edge, giving very high pressure. Force is measured in units called newtons, after scientist Isaac Newton *(see opposite)*. Pressure is measured in newtons per square meter.

17

MOTION

MOTION is any kind of movement. Motion is caused by forces. A still or stationary object does not move unless a force acts on it to start it going. Once it is moving it carries on at the same speed in a straight line unless a force makes it speed up, change direction or slow down and stop.

An object stays still or keeps moving in a straight line, unless forces act on it. A bus will not start to move unless the engine provides a force to make it do so. This tendency of an object's motion to stay the same is called inertia. Once the bus is moving, the force of air resistance tries to slow it down. The engine keeps the bus going forward. If the bus stops suddenly, people on it fall forward because there is nothing to stop them moving.

There are many kinds of movement. An object going in a straight line like a rocket shooting through deep space has linear motion. An object going around a central point like a ball swung around on a string has circular motion. An object moving to and fro like a pendulum has reciprocating motion. An object that twists around like a wheel or a screwdriver has rotary motion.

FRICTION

When two objects that are touching try to move past each other, they rub against each other. This produces a force called friction which tries to stop the movement. If the surfaces of the objects are rough, like sandpaper, then friction is greater. If they are smooth and slippery, especially if lubricated with oil or grease, then friction is less. Friction is "the enemy of machines": It opposes movement, causes wear and tear, and changes useful energy into waste heat. But friction can also be helpful. A vehicle slows down suddenly because of friction provided by its brakes. A bulldozer's tracks dig into the earth with so much friction that they cannot slip *(above)*. So the bulldozer can push huge mounds of soil.

People on a "Chair-o-Plane" ride *(left)* have several forces acting on them. As always, Earth's gravity pulls them down toward the ground. The chair holds them up and pushes them forward. Its cable pulls them around in a circle.

A skier slides easily over snow and ice because the skis press down and rub hard on them. The friction makes them heat and melt into water, which is very slippery with low friction. After the skis have past, the snow and ice freeze again.

MACHINES

OUR WORLD runs on machines. They make work easier for us. A machine uses physical efforts, forces, and work to get a job done. It can be as complicated as a jet engine or a combine harvester to gather crops. Yet it can be as simple as a crowbar used to lift heavy stones or a wheel on an old cart. Even the most complicated machines are combinations of a few kinds of simple machines.

Ancient structures like the Egyptian pyramids *(left)* were built using simple machines such as ramps and rollers. The driving force came from humans. The ground drill, or auger *(above)*, is a modern machine, an engine-driven screw.

A rope and pulley *(left)* changes the direction of a pulling force. It is usually easier to pull down on a rope than to pull up. Loop the rope around two pulleys and it can lift a heavier weight than with one. But the rope must be pulled further. Adding more pulleys to the system makes the lifting even easier, but the rope has to be pulled even further. The total work done to move the weight is the same in each case.

Pulley

A lever is a stiff bar that pivots at a fulcrum. If the fulcrum is near one end then a small force at the other end moves a heavy weight but not very far.

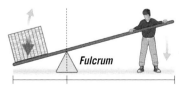

Fulcrum

The main kinds of simple machines are:
- **Inclined plane** A slope or ramp to drag or roll heavy objects upward.
- **Wedge** Two ramps back to back as used in knife and ax blades.
- **Lever** A rigid bar or beam that pivots on a hinge or fulcrum, like a crowbar.
- **Screw** A wedge twisted into a corkscrew shape forces its way through a substance.
- **Wheel and axle** An endless curved ramp, the wheel, turning on its central point, the axle.
- **Pulley** A wheel with a groove in its rim for a rope, chain or cable.

These machines make tasks easier. But they do not give something for nothing. Usually the task takes longer and involves more movement, so the total work at the end is the same as doing the task without it.

ENERGY

ENERGY is the ability to make things happen, cause changes, and carry out work. Any change anywhere in the universe, from a tiny meteorite hitting a planet to an exploding star, means that energy is at work. In daily life, energy is all around us in many different forms. Light and sound energy travel through the air as waves. Heat is a form known as thermal energy. Movement or motion is, too, and is called kinetic energy. Objects even have energy because of their place or position. This is called potential energy. A boulder on a hilltop has potential energy because gravity tries to pull it down. As the boulder begins to roll its potential energy changes into kinetic energy.

Energy is all around, present in different forms and changing from one form to another. Without energy our world would be completely dark, cold, still, and silent.

Energy from the Sun bathes our world. It is in two main forms, light and heat. It takes more than 8 minutes to travel nearly 93,210,000 miles (150 million km) through space to Earth.

Energy can cause changes and it can change itself. It can convert between one form and another. The boulder rolls down the hill, converting some of its potential energy to kinetic energy. Water also flows downhill with kinetic energy. We can harness this kinetic energy in a hydroelectric power station and convert it into electrical energy (see page 30), yet another form of energy. Electricity is very useful in our modern world. It can be transported long distances along wires. It can be converted to other forms of energy, like light from a light bulb, heat in an electric kettle and sound from a loudspeaker.

Matter contains chemical energy, in the links or bonds between atoms (see page 12). The bonds need energy to form and they release this energy when they are broken. We make use of chemical energy in fuels such as petrol. The bonds break as the fuel burns and releases heat.

The human body needs energy to drive its life processes like heartbeat, breathing, and movement. The energy is present in chemical form as the nutrients in our food. We digest the food to obtain the energy and store it as body starches and sugars.

Chemical energy in the body in the form of blood sugar is taken to muscles. The muscles convert it into the energy of motion so we can move about.

CONSERVING ENERGY

Energy can be changed or converted from one form to another. But it is never destroyed or created, lost or gained. It is conserved—the amount stays the same. At the end of a process or event, the total amount of energy is the same as at the beginning. For example, the chemical energy in a car's gasoline is converted into the same amount of energy as the car's motion, heat, and sound. The principle of energy conservation means the total amount of energy in the universe is always the same.

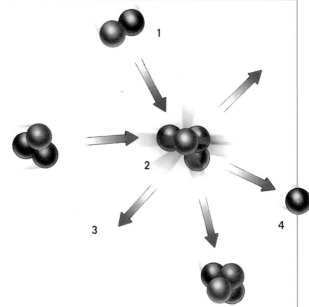

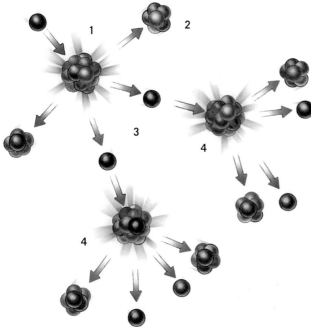

Another form of energy is matter itself. Matter can be converted into energy and energy can be changed into matter. This conversion is used in nuclear power stations (see above). A nuclear particle called a neutron smashes into the nucleus of a uranium atom (1). The nucleus breaks into two parts (2). This releases large amounts of heat and other energy and also two more fast-moving neutrons (3). These smash into more uranium nuclei and so on in a chain reaction (4). Splitting of nuclei is known as nuclear fission. During the process bits of matter cease to exist and become vast quantities of energy instead.

A similar process of changing matter into energy happens naturally in the Sun *(above)*. The Sun is made mainly of hydrogen. Tremendous temperatures and pressures at its center squeeze or fuse together the nuclei of the atoms (1) to form the nucleus of a helium atom (2). Vast amounts of energy are given off (3) which emerge from the Sun mainly as light and heat. A neutron may also be given off to continue the reaction (4). Since the nuclei join or fuse, this is called nuclear fusion. Compared to fission used in our nuclear power stations, fusion power would cause less radioactive wastes and pollution. Fusion power may be the energy source of the future.

Geothermal energy from hot rocks deep in the earth causes geysers, jets of hot water and steam. This form of energy will last millions of years.

SOUND

ONE OF THE MOST familiar forms of energy in daily life is sound. We hear natural sounds like birdsong and wind. We hear the noise of vehicles and machines, and sounds such as speech and music from radios, televisions, and stereo systems. We also rely on sounds to communicate when we talk to others.

Sounds are made by objects that vibrate (move to and fro rapidly). As an object vibrates, it alternately pushes and pulls at the air around it. The air is squashed and stretched as the molecules of the gases in air are pressed close together and then pulled farther apart. These are regions of high and low air pressure. They pass outward away from the object in all directions. They are called sound waves.

Sound waves travel out from their source as peaks and troughs like ripples on a pond. But sound spreads in all directions, rather than just horizontally as on a pond.

Sound waves start as the energy of movement in the vibrations. This is transferred to the energy of movement in air molecules. As the sound waves spread out they widen and disperse, like the ripples on a pond after a stone is thrown in. So the sound gradually gets weaker and fades away. However if there is a hard, smooth surface in the way, such as a wall, then some sound waves bounce off it and come back again. The bouncing is known as reflection and we hear the returning sound as an echo.

An object that vibrates to produce sound waves is a sound source. A bow rubs over the cello's string and makes it vibrate. The vibrations pass into the air and also to the cello's hollow body making the sound louder and richer.

Sea water (5,020 feet per second)

Air (1,125 feet per second)

Steel (16,570 feet per second)

The speed of sound varies depending on the substance it travels through. Atoms in steel are closer than molecules in air, so the vibrations of sound move faster and further.

Sounds also travel as vibrations through liquids, such as water, and solids, such as metals. The atoms or molecules are closer together in liquids than in air, and even closer still in solids. So sounds travel through them much faster.

PITCH AND VOLUME

Sound has two important features *(see chart below)*. One is pitch. A low-pitched sound is deep, like a roll of thunder or a booming big drum. A high-pitched sound is shrill, like a snake's hiss or the tinkle of a triangle. Pitch depends on the frequency of sound waves—the number of waves per second. High-pitched sounds have high frequencies.

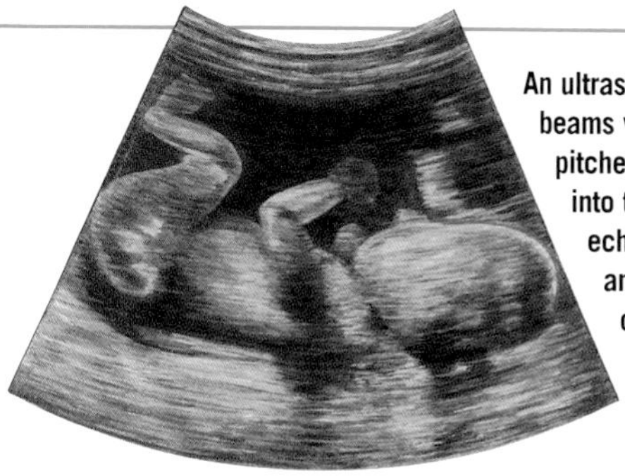

An ultrasound scanner beams very high-pitched sound waves into the body. The echoes are analyzed by a computer to form an image, like this baby in the womb.

Some sounds are so high pitched that our ears cannot detect them. They are known as ultrasounds. Many animals, like dogs and bats, can hear ultrasounds.

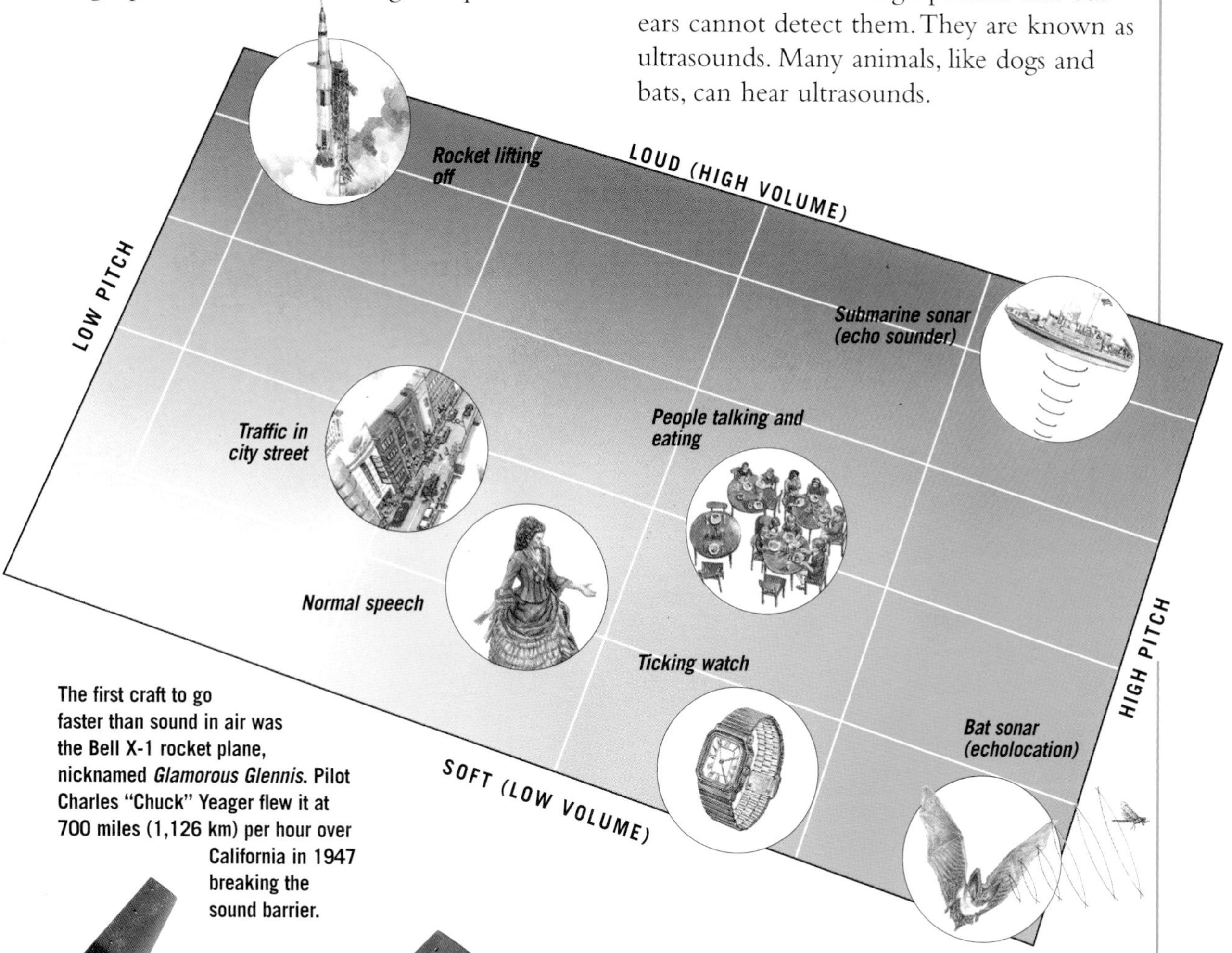

LOW PITCH

LOUD (HIGH VOLUME)

Rocket lifting off

Submarine sonar (echo sounder)

Traffic in city street

People talking and eating

Normal speech

Ticking watch

HIGH PITCH

Bat sonar (echolocation)

The first craft to go faster than sound in air was the Bell X-1 rocket plane, nicknamed *Glamorous Glennis*. Pilot Charles "Chuck" Yeager flew it at 700 miles (1,126 km) per hour over California in 1947 breaking the sound barrier.

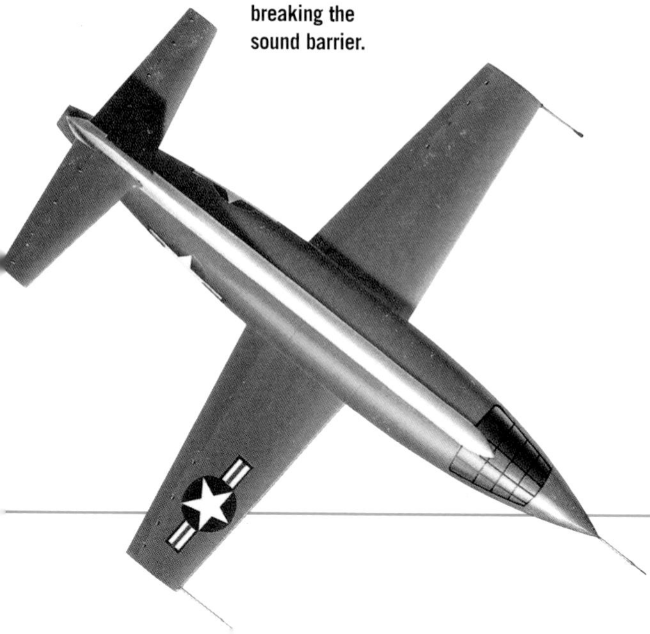

SOFT (LOW VOLUME)

The second important feature of sound is its loudness or volume. Some sounds are so quiet that we can only just hear them, like a ticking watch or the rustling of leaves. Other sounds are so loud, like the roar of engines or the powerful music in a disco, that they may damage the ears. Sound volume, or intensity, is measured in units called decibels (dB). Sounds of more than 80 to 90 decibels can damage our hearing.

HEAT

HOW WARM is the weather today? It may be cold and wintry or hot and summery. Heat is a vital part of our lives. We need to keep our bodies comfortably warm with clothing, especially in cold conditions. If body temperature falls from its normal 98.6°F (37°C) to below about 86°F (30°C), fatal hypothermia may set in.

A spacecraft reentering Earth's atmosphere glows red with heat. The friction with air generates tremendous heat that is resisted by special insulating heat shield.

We cook our food with heat using gas or electricity. Countless machines and industrial processes use heat, from making pottery or a photocopy to a steelworks or power station. Heat is also given off as a waste form of energy by many processes. In a power station most of the heat is used to generate electricity, but some is released as clouds of steam from huge cooling towers.

Heat almost any solid and it will eventually melt into a liquid. Even solid rocks melt or become molten at above about 1,472-1,832°F (800-1,000°C). The liquid rock that oozes or spurts from volcanoes is called lava. The temperature and pressure inside some volcanoes are so great that some types of rock not only melt, they boil and bubble as they give off the gases trapped inside them.

Heat is a type of energy—the vibrations of atoms and molecules. The more an atom moves or vibrates, the more heat or thermal energy it has. In a solid, the atoms have fixed central positions but each atom vibrates slightly about its central position, like a ball tied to a nail by elastic. Heat the solid and the atoms vibrate more. When they have enough vibrations, the atoms break from their fixed positions (the "elastic" snaps), and they move about at random. The solid has melted into a liquid. Heat it more and the atoms fly further apart. The liquid becomes a gas.

Human beings are suited to temperatures of about 68 to 77°F (20-25°C). We cope with warmer or colder conditions by wearing suitable clothes. Lacking clothes, whales use a thick layer of body fat called blubber under the skin to keep in their body heat in the cold sea.

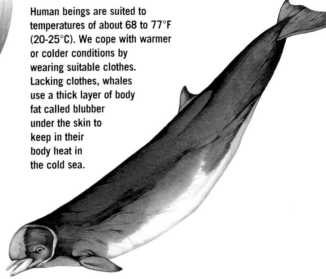

TEMPERATURE

Cold is not the presence of something that opposes heat, but simply the lack of heat. Temperature is not the same as heat. Heat is a form of energy, while temperature is a measure of how much heat energy a substance or object contains. A slice of apple pie at 104°F (40°C) contains more heat energy than a same-sized slice of the same pie at 86°F (30°C). We can judge its temperature quite accurately when we touch the slice with our skin, and especially with our fingertips or lips. But this judgement is only safe within a certain range. Temperatures greater than about 122°F (50°C) or lower than about 14°F (-10°C) cause pain and may damage the skin. We measure temperatures accurately using devices called thermometers.

Birds glide and soar in the convection currents rising from areas of sea and land warmed by the Sun.

The third way that heat moves is by radiation. It is in the form of infrared waves which are part of a whole range of waves, including radio waves, light, and X rays, known as the electromagnetic spectrum. Conduction and convection both need matter to transfer heat. Radiation does not. Infrared waves can pass through space, which is how the Sun's heat reaches Earth.

HOW HEAT MOVES

Heat can move around and between objects in three main ways. One is conduction, when heat energy passes between two objects in physical contact. When you touch an object to see how warm it is, you receive some of its heat by conduction. A second way is by convection. This only happens in liquids and gases. As some of the atoms or molecules receive heat energy and become warm they spread out more. The heated part of the liquid or solid is now less dense than its cooler surroundings so it rises or floats *(see page 5)*. As it rises, it carries its heat energy in the form of a convection current. You can feel this as warm air rising from a central heating radiator.

As satellites orbit Earth they come into the full glare and heat of the Sun. Shiny foil reflects the heat (infrared) waves from the Sun and keeps the craft cooler.

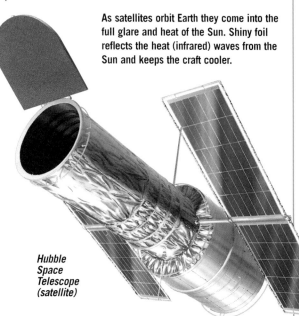

Hubble Space Telescope (satellite)

Like light waves, infrared waves reflect from light-colored or shiny surfaces. On a hot day, light-colored clothes reflect the Sun's warmth and keep you cooler than dark clothing, which absorbs the warmth. Substances that slow down conduction and convection, such as wood, plastic, and glass fiber, are called thermal insulators. Layers of fat, or blubber in a whale *(see opposite),* are good insulators.

The faster an aircraft goes, the greater the heat from friction with air. Very fast planes like the X-15 rocket have special heat-radiating paint that gives out heat as fast as possible, to prevent the metal skin of the plane melting at high speed.

LIGHT

LIGHT is a kind of energy *(see page 20)*. It is the form of energy that our eyes can detect, enabling us to see. It is produced by very hot things—the Sun, fire, and the tiny wire inside electric lightbulbs. Certain animals also have light-producing organs.

Light from the Sun is essential to life on Earth. Some creatures live off minerals in the ocean depths but these are exceptions. Most plants use sunlight to make their food. All plant-eating animals, together with other animals that eat plant eaters, also therefore depend on sunlight.

Light rays can only travel in straight lines. If they strike an object which does not allow light to pass through it (an opaque object), a shadow is cast on the unlit side. Light can be reflected, however. Light reflected from objects allows us to see them. Light rays strike and bounce off a flat, shiny surface like a mirror at the same angle. This enables us to see our reflection.

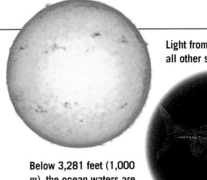

Light from the Sun drowns out all other stars during the day.

Below 3,281 feet (1,000 m), the ocean waters are completely without light. Here, fish have special light-producing organs.

THE SPEED OF LIGHT

When we switch on an electric light, it seems that the room is filled with light instantaneously. But light rays do take time to travel from their source. They travel extremely quickly: about 186,400 miles (300,000 km) (or seven-and-a-half times around the world) per second in outer space. The speed of light is, in fact, the speed limit for the universe: Nothing can travel faster. Light waves are able to travel through empty space—a vacuum—whereas sound waves *(see page 22)* cannot. Light actually moves less quickly through air, water, or glass than through empty space.

Because stars are very far from Earth—at least thousands of billions of miles—astronomers measure their distances in light years, the amount of time it takes for light to travel to us from them *(see page 32)*.

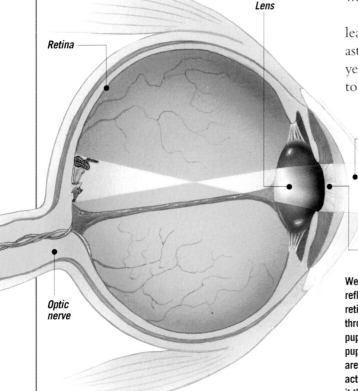

Retina

Lens

Cornea

Light rays

Pupil

Optic nerve

We see an object when light reflected from it falls on the retina of the eye. Light passes through the black part of the eye, actually a hole called the pupil. The cornea and convex lens *(see opposite)* behind the pupil focuses the image onto the retina. From here, messages are carried to the brain by the optic nerve. (The image is actually focused upside down onto the retina. The brain turns it the right way up again.)

An electric lightbulb contains a filament made of tungsten, wound in a tight coil. When electricity passes through the coil it becomes white hot (about 4,532°F). Argon gas in the bulb prevents the filament from burning out.

Some animals are able to produce light, a feature called bioluminescence. It is generated by chemical reactions in living cells. Female glowworms (really beetles, *right*) emit light when they are ready to mate.

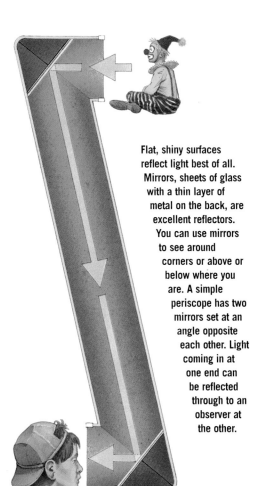

Flat, shiny surfaces reflect light best of all. Mirrors, sheets of glass with a thin layer of metal on the back, are excellent reflectors. You can use mirrors to see around corners or above or below where you are. A simple periscope has two mirrors set at an angle opposite each other. Light coming in at one end can be reflected through to an observer at the other.

REFRACTION OF LIGHT

Light rays bend, or refract, when they pass through different transparent materials. This is because light travels at different speeds through different materials. At the boundary between two materials, for example air and water, the light changes speed slightly and is refracted from its straight path. You can see this effect when looking at the bottom of swimming pool. It looks much shallower than it really is.

FOCUSING LIGHT

A lens, a shaped piece of glass or plastic, can bend light, either spreading it out or bringing it closer together. A convex lens, one that is thicker in the middle than at the edge, brings light rays together at a single point called a focus. The eye contains a natural convex lens which focuses an image onto the retina at the back of the eye. If you hold a convex lens so that the object you are looking at lies between the lens and the focus, the object will appear larger and further from the lens than it really is. A simple magnifying glass *(above)* is a convex lens, and is useful for studying minute detail as, for example, on a postage stamp or a tiny insect or flower.

A concave lens is the opposite of a convex lens: It is thicker around the edge than in the middle. This kind of lens diverges (spreads out) light rays. It is used in glasses to correct shortsightedness.

COLOR

ONE OF THE MAIN features of light *(see page 26)* is color. If light were just pure white, our whole world would be black and white and shades of gray. But white light is not pure. It is a mixture of all the colors of the rainbow which are known as the spectrum of light.

Colors exist because light is in the form of waves and not all the waves have the same wavelength. Some are slightly longer than others, and these we see as red. Light waves of medium wavelength appear to our eyes as green. We see the shortest light waves as violet. A leaf is green because its surface absorbs all the colors in white light except green, which it reflects into our eyes. A red flag absorbs all colors except red. Objects that reflect all colors are white.

A rainbow forms across the sky when the Sun shines from behind you at rain falling in front of you.

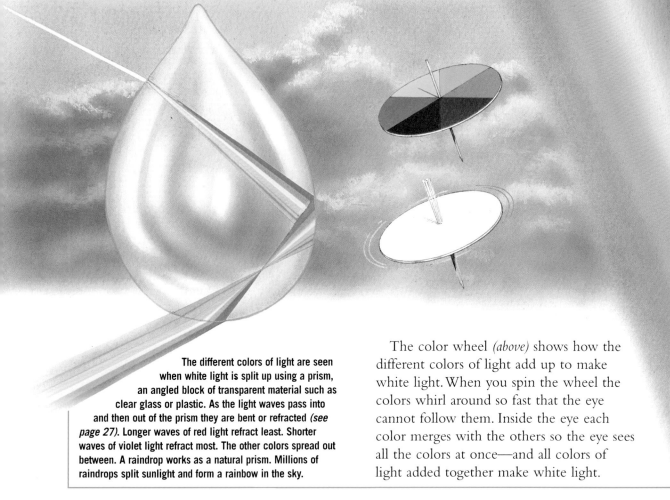

The different colors of light are seen when white light is split up using a prism, an angled block of transparent material such as clear glass or plastic. As the light waves pass into and then out of the prism they are bent or refracted *(see page 27)*. Longer waves of red light refract least. Shorter waves of violet light refract most. The other colors spread out between. A raindrop works as a natural prism. Millions of raindrops split sunlight and form a rainbow in the sky.

The color wheel *(above)* shows how the different colors of light add up to make white light. When you spin the wheel the colors whirl around so fast that the eye cannot follow them. Inside the eye each color merges with the others so the eye sees all the colors at once—and all colors of light added together make white light.

28

The three primary colors of light add together to make white light.

ADDING COLORS

We see colors in books like this, and on screens such as the television, in different ways. A television or computer screen has thousands of tiny dots that glow and give out light. These dots have actually only three colors—red, green, and blue. These colors are known as the primary colors of light. Added to each other in different combinations and brightness they can make any other color. For example, red and green together make the color yellow. Red and blue produce the pink color known as magenta. Blue and green form cyan, a type of turquoise. The three primary colors of red, blue, and green added together make white light.

On the screen of a computer or TV the dots are arranged in groups known as pixels. The different colors of dots flash on and off in different combinations and shine with different brightnesses. From a distance, the eye cannot see the individual dots. They merge to produce larger areas of color. When all the red dots on an area of the screen shine, that area looks red. When all three colors of dots in an area of the screen shine brightly, that area looks white. Also the dots flash on and off many times each second, again too fast for the eye to follow. So they merge together in time to produce multicolored, moving pictures.

SUBTRACTING COLORS

Colored pictures in a book are made like those on a screen, using tiny colored dots that merge together. The dots are inks made with colored substances called pigments. There are three primary pigment colors— yellow, magenta and cyan. They work in the opposite way of light colors. They do not add together, but take away or subtract. A yellow dot takes away all colors of light except yellow which it reflects. The other two dots do the same for their colors. By taking away individual colors, the dots merge to produce areas of other colors. All three dots together make black.

The wolf's mask *(below)* is realistic and frightening. Yet it is printed using tiny dots of only three colors. They can be separated as magenta, cyan, and yellow *(above)*. To save on colored inks some parts of the page, like these words, are printed with ready-made black ink *(left)*.

ELECTRICITY

ONE OF THE MOST useful forms of energy in today's world is electricity. It is transportable, which means it can be carried long distances by wires and cables. It is convertible, being changed into many other forms of energy, such as light from an electric lightbulb, and movement in an electric motor. It is also controllable. We can turn it on and off with a switch, or up and down with a knob. When a city suffers a power outage and falls still and silent, we realize how much we depend on electricity.

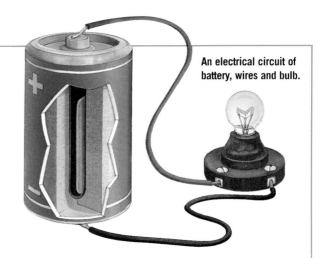

An electrical circuit of battery, wires and bulb.

Electricity is the movement of electrons, the negative particles around the nucleus of an atom *(see page 6)*. Most metals, especially silver and copper, have electrons that can move easily from atom to atom, so they are good carriers or conductors of electricity. Electrons are pushed along the conductor by a battery or generator. But they flow only if they have a complete pathway of conductors called a circuit *(above)*. Flowing electricity is known as electric current.

In substances such as rocks, wood, plastics, rubber, and glass the electrons do not move easily. These materials prevent the flow of electricity and are known as insulators, but they may gain or lose electrons on their surface as a static electric charge *(below)*.

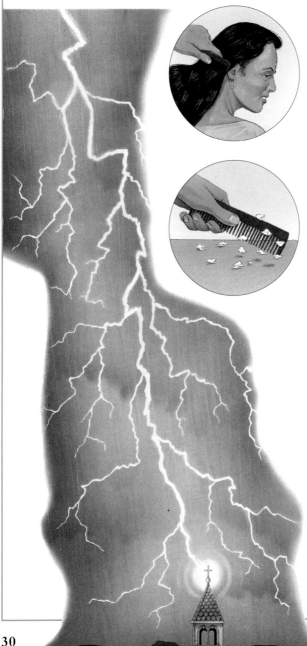

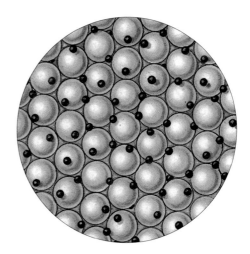

Static electricity is produced when electrons are separated from their atoms. On a comb it attracts bits of paper. In the sky it causes lightning!

Electric current flows along a wire as electrons that detach from the outermost parts of their own atoms and jump or hop along to the next available atoms.

MAGNETISM

WE CANNOT SEE or feel the force of magnetism. But it is all around us since Earth is itself a giant magnet. A magnetic force affects mainly objects and substances that contain the metal iron. It pulls or attracts them. The force is present as a magnetic field around a magnet, which is itself usually made of iron.

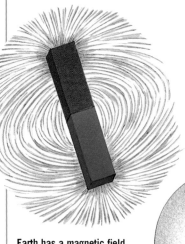

A bar magnet is a strip of iron or steel in which the atoms are lined up in a certain way. Its magnetic force is strongest at its two ends or poles.

Earth has a magnetic field and two magnetic poles, north and south, almost as if it had a giant bar magnet inside.

A magnetic compass is a needle-shaped magnet. Its poles are attracted to Earth's poles so it always turns to point north-south.

Magnets of different sizes and shapes have hundreds of uses, from holding notes on a refrigerator to being vital parts in electrical generators, motors, and loudspeakers.

A magnet does not always attract another magnet. Its magnetic force is strongest at two areas called its poles. These are different from each other and known as north and south poles. The north pole of one magnet attracts the south pole of another magnet. But it pushes away or repels the other magnet's north pole. The general rule is that unlike poles attract, like poles repel.

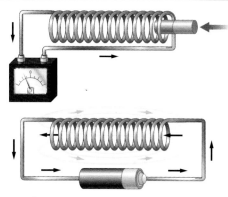

ELECTROMAGNETISM

Electricity and magnetism are two aspects of the same force, called the electromagnetic force. They are so closely linked that one can produce the other. A magnetic field moving near a wire causes electricity to flow in the wire *(top)*. An electric current flowing in a wire makes a magnetic field around the wire *(above)*. Twist the wire into a coil and it produces a stronger magnetic field. It can be turned on and off by switching the electricity on and off. This is an electromagnet. Electromagnetism is the basis of electric motors and generators.

A maglev (magnetic levitation) train uses the pushing force between the like poles of magnets in the train and track. The force holds the wheel-less train above the track.

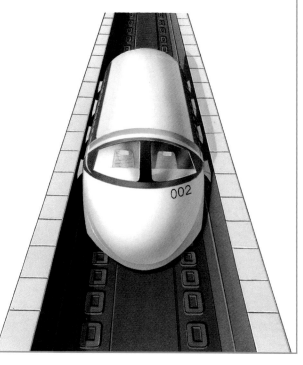

UNIVERSE

EVERYTHING that we can think of—and everything else that exists—all belong to the universe. From grains of sand to tall buildings, from particles of dust to giant stars and planets, from microscopic bacteria to people—all are part of the universe. It even includes empty space.

The universe is unimaginably vast: billions upon billions of miles wide. Distances in the universe are so great that we have to use a special measure to record them. This is a light year, or the distance that light, which moves at a speed of about 186,400 miles (300,000 km) per second, travels in one year: about 5,878,000,000,000 miles (9,460,528,405,000 km). The nearest star to Earth (after the Sun), Proxima Centauri, is 4.2 light years away. The most distant objects we know in the universe are more than 13 billion light years away from Earth.

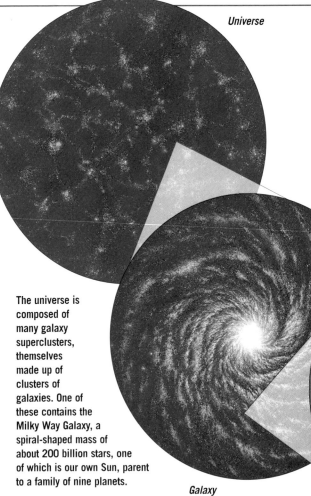

Universe

The universe is composed of many galaxy superclusters, themselves made up of clusters of galaxies. One of these contains the Milky Way Galaxy, a spiral-shaped mass of about 200 billion stars, one of which is our own Sun, parent to a family of nine planets.

Galaxy

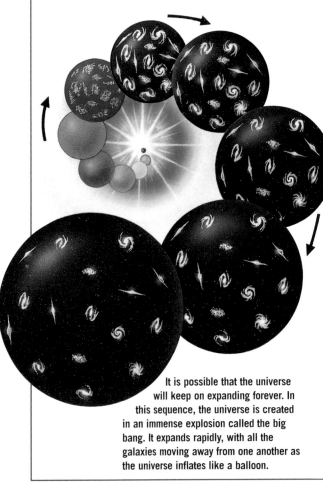

It is possible that the universe will keep on expanding forever. In this sequence, the universe is created in an immense explosion called the big bang. It expands rapidly, with all the galaxies moving away from one another as the universe inflates like a balloon.

Nearly all the matter in the universe is contained in galaxies, enormous masses of stars, gas, and dust *(see page 34)*. There may be about about 100 billion galaxies, each containing hundreds of billions of stars. Galaxies are grouped into giant "clouds" of galaxies, called superclusters. These are spread around the universe like a net, made up of strings and knots. In between there are gigantic empty spaces.

The superclusters are, themselves, made up of smaller clusters of galaxies. One of these, a cluster of 30 galaxies or so, is called the Local Group. It contains the Milky Way Galaxy, the vast spiral of stars to which our own local star, the Sun, belongs.

Astronomers have discovered that all galaxies are rushing away from one another. This means that, a long time ago, they were once all close together. So the universe had a definite beginning—and may have an end.

Living environment

Earth and Moon

Solar System

The third planet from the Sun is Earth, orbited by the Moon. Earth is the only world in the universe where life is *known* to exist, but we may discover others one day.

About a billion years after the big bang, the clouds of gas started to form into galaxies. Matter inside the galaxies went on clumping together until stars were created *(see page 35)*. Our own Sun was born in this way about 5 billion years ago. Its family of planets, including our Earth, was formed from the debris spinning round the infant Sun *(see page 45)*. With billions and billions of stars and planets forming in the same way across the universe, it seems almost certain that life will have also evolved elsewhere. Will we on Earth one day make contact with these alien life-forms?

The expansion of the universe is slowing down. Some astronomers think that gravity may eventually bring the expansion to a halt, then collapse all matter once more to a single point in a "Big Crunch." Others believe that there is not enough material in the universe to do this and that the universe will carry on expanding forever.

BIG BANG

Many astronomers believe that the universe began life in a single momentous event. This was an incredibly hot, dense explosion called the big bang, which took place about 15 billion years ago. During this explosion, all matter, energy, space—and time itself— were created.

In the first few millionths of a second, the particles that make up atoms, the building blocks of all matter *(see page 6),* were formed. It took about 100,000 years for the first atoms, those of the gases hydrogen and helium, to come together. By this time, the searing heat of the big bang had cooled, space had expanded, and the gases began to spread out. Gradually, however, gravity *(see page 16)* drew the gases together, leaving vast regions of empty space in between.

Many scientists think that all matter in the universe will eventually collide: the "Big Crunch." Vast amounts of invisible "dark matter" in the universe may exert sufficient gravity to halt its expansion and cause the galaxies to compress together.

GALAXIES

GALAXIES are gigantic collections of stars. The galaxy in which the Sun is situated, the Milky Way Galaxy, is a vast spiral of about 200 billion stars measuring about 100,000 light years across. There are billions more galaxies in the universe, most of which are elliptical (oval) in shape. There are also others that have irregular shapes.

The Milky Way has a bulge at its center, the nucleus, where older red stars are concentrated. Four giant arms radiate out from the nucleus. These contain younger blue stars as well as areas of gas and dust—the raw material for the creation of new stars. The whole spiral spins at a speed of about 155 miles (250 km) per second.

The Horsehead Nebula is really a gigantic cloud of dust and gas that has taken on a familiar shape. It is one of many clouds in our galaxy where stars start to form.

The Milky Way Galaxy closely resembles the Andromeda Galaxy, which lies 2.25 million light years away. The Sun is situated on one of the spiral arms about halfway out from the nucleus. Here are mostly yellow and orange young-to-middle aged stars.

This illustration *(below)* is a view of the Milky Way Galaxy seen from the side. It looks like a pair of fried eggs stuck together back-to-back. The "yolks" form the central bulge, or nucleus, while the "whites" form the spiral-shaped, flattened disc surrounding it. The Sun lies about 25,000 light years (halfway out) from the central point.

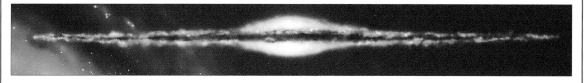

STARS

STARS are giant spinning balls of hot gases. Like massive nuclear power stations, they produce vast amounts of energy in the form of heat and light, which they radiate across space as they shine.

They may look like tiny points of light in the night sky, but many stars are incredibly big. Betelgeuse, in the constellation of Orion, is 800 times the size of the Sun, our local star. Stars vary enormously according to the amount of light they emit. Some of the most powerful give off more than 100,000 times the light of the Sun, while others are 100,000 times weaker.

Stars are born when clouds of dust and gas in space, known as nebulae, compress together under the force of gravity to become dense "blobs," called protostars. It is not certain why this happens. Maybe the pressure of an exploding star nearby at the end of its life triggers the process.

After a star has formed it becomes a stable "main sequence" star. The Sun is a typical star of average brightness. More massive stars, like Rigel (also in Orion), glow blue-white, while at the other end of the scale, a white dwarf, the collapsed core of an old star, is no bigger than Earth.

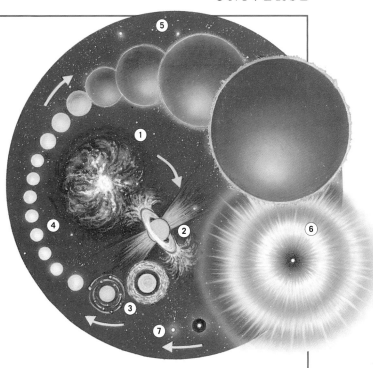

A star begins its life as a dense mass of gas and dust called a protostar (1). The core becomes so hot that nuclear reactions *(see page 21)* start deep inside it. Gas and dust are blown away (2), although some remain in a disc surrounding the new star. Planets may form here (3). The star is now a main sequence star (4). When the fuel it uses to produce energy runs out, the core collapses and the star swells into a red giant (5). A massive star will become a supergiant that will blast apart in a mighty explosion called a supernova (6). It ends its days as a neutron star or a black hole (7). A red giant will puff away into space, leaving behind a white dwarf.

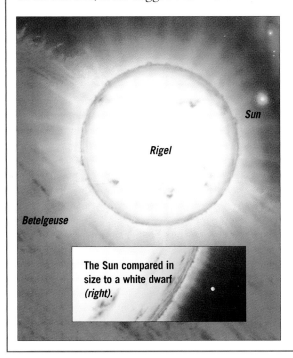

Sun

Rigel

Betelgeuse

The Sun compared in size to a white dwarf (right).

A red giant's outer layers eventually flake off into space, leaving a planetary nebula (right). A supergiant goes out in a supernova. The Crab Nebula is the remains of one (below).

BLACK HOLES

BLACK HOLES are the strangest objects in the universe. No one has ever seen one, but most astronomers are convinced that they exist. They are tiny regions of space surrounded by a force of gravity so strong that nothing, not even light, can escape from them.

All bodies in space exert a force of gravity, the force which attracts other things toward them *(see page 16)*. The greater an object, the stronger its gravitational pull, and the harder it is to escape from it. A rocket launched from Earth must go faster than 24,850 miles (40,000 km) per hour (its "escape velocity") to escape Earth's gravitational pull. The Sun is many thousands of times more massive than Earth, so a rocket would have to travel much faster—more than 1,243,000 miles (2 million km) per hour. If there was an object much bigger or denser than the Sun, an escape velocity equal to that of the speed of light may be needed to escape from it.

Where might an object of such high density be found? Stars more than 10 times as heavy as the Sun burn up their fuel in a much shorter time—a few million years, compared to the Sun's 10 billion years. They swell into massive supergiants before blasting apart in supernovas *(see page 35)*. A supernova's core compresses in seconds to a

Billions of light years away, a huge disc of gas and dust swirls around a giant black hole at the core of a quasar. The incredible energy blasts two jets of particles—the component parts of atoms—out into space.

tiny, super-dense body called a neutron star. If it weighs more than three Suns, it squeezes further. An escape velocity of the speed of light would be needed to travel away from it. Any light rays would be pulled back in, so the object is invisible—a black hole.

EINSTEIN'S GENERAL THEORY

The great German physicist Albert Einstein (1879–1955) found another way to explain how space, light, and matter would behave close to a black hole. In his general theory of relativity of 1915, Einstein proposed that the gravitational pull of an object would result in the "curving" of space, in the same way that a person can curve a trampoline. A massive object creates a large "dent" in space into which light and matter would fall. The denser the object, the greater the dent. So the Sun would make only a shallow dent, whereas a neutron star would create a very deep dent. A black hole, the densest object of all, creates a dent so deep that nothing can escape from it.

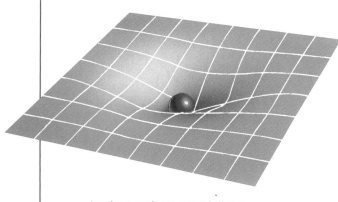

Imagine a star in space as a ball on a rubber sheet. A massive object like a star will "bend" space and anything close to it will fall in toward it. If the ball were so heavy that the sheet stretched into a long, deep tube, the result would be a black hole.

QUASARS

Incredibly powerful, massive black holes may, astronomers think, be found lurking at the centers of galaxies. There could even be one at the center of our own Milky Way Galaxy. Astronomers have detected a ring of fast-moving, hot gas swirling around the center. The ring of gas is probably in the grip of a powerful gravitational pull—most likely, astronomers suspect, to be the work of a black hole.

The activity at the center of our galaxy is as nothing compared to that of quasars. These objects look like stars, but they lie at incredible distances from us: the farthest quasars are 13 billion light years away. To be visible at that distance means they must be giving off immense amounts of energy. Quasars are the centers of extremely violent galaxies containing supermassive black holes, weighing up to 100 billion Suns. The brilliant light comes from the disc of hot gas and dust spiralling into the black hole.

To Albert Einstein, gravity was a property of space and not a force between objects.

Black holes are invisible, but it is possible to detect them by studying their effects. Astronomers observing a star called Cygnus X-1 saw that it was giving off enormous amounts of energy (a sure sign of violent activity in the universe). They discovered that this huge, hot blue star was being dragged around in a circle by an unseen object with a huge gravitational pull. That unseen object, astronomers now believe, is a black hole, which is tearing gas from the star. The gas forms a whirling disc before plummeting into the black hole. As it falls, it travels faster and faster until it moves almost at the speed of light itself. Close to the hole, the gas becomes so hot it emits massive amounts of energy.

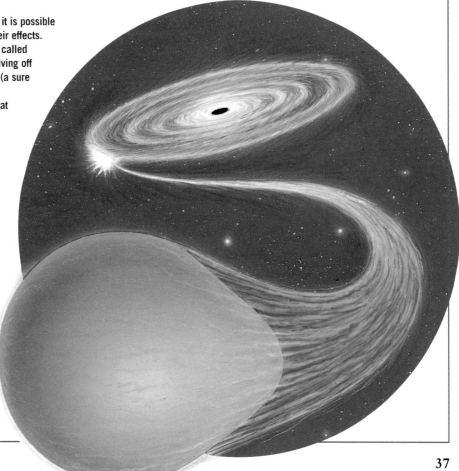

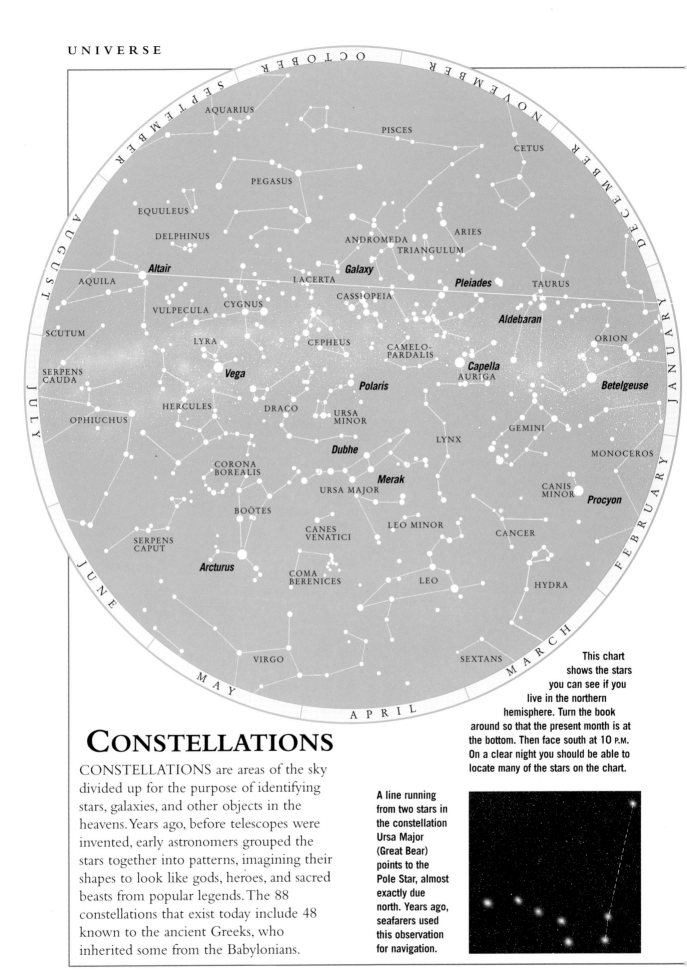

This chart shows the stars you can see if you live in the northern hemisphere. Turn the book around so that the present month is at the bottom. Then face south at 10 P.M. On a clear night you should be able to locate many of the stars on the chart.

CONSTELLATIONS

CONSTELLATIONS are areas of the sky divided up for the purpose of identifying stars, galaxies, and other objects in the heavens. Years ago, before telescopes were invented, early astronomers grouped the stars together into patterns, imagining their shapes to look like gods, heroes, and sacred beasts from popular legends. The 88 constellations that exist today include 48 known to the ancient Greeks, who inherited some from the Babylonians.

A line running from two stars in the constellation Ursa Major (Great Bear) points to the Pole Star, almost exactly due north. Years ago, seafarers used this observation for navigation.

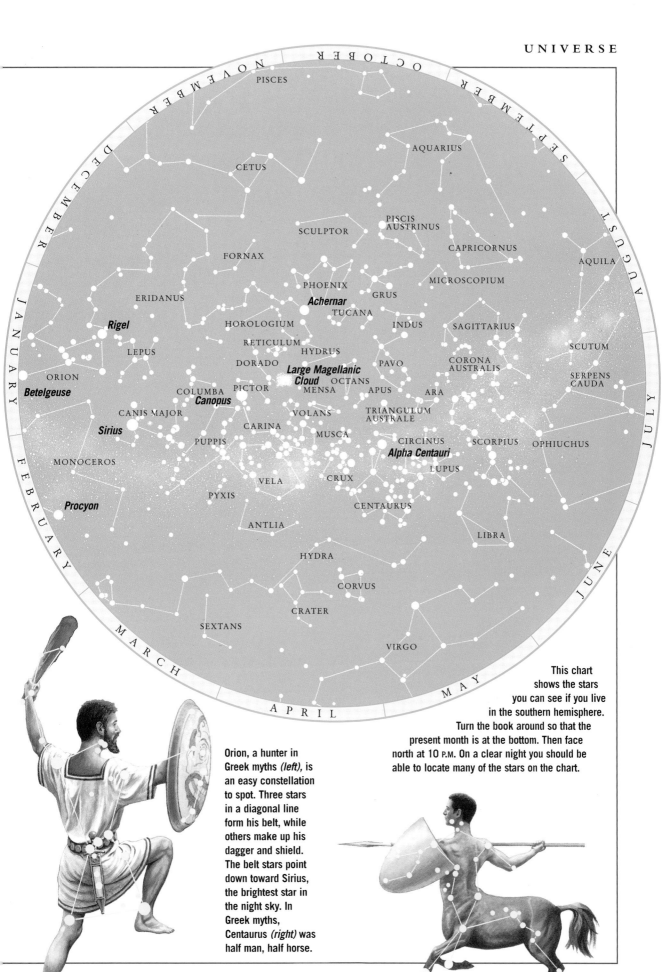

This chart shows the stars you can see if you live in the southern hemisphere. Turn the book around so that the present month is at the bottom. Then face north at 10 P.M. On a clear night you should be able to locate many of the stars on the chart.

Orion, a hunter in Greek myths *(left)*, is an easy constellation to spot. Three stars in a diagonal line form his belt, while others make up his dagger and shield. The belt stars point down toward Sirius, the brightest star in the night sky. In Greek myths, Centaurus *(right)* was half man, half horse.

39

SOLAR SYSTEM

THE SOLAR SYSTEM consists of the Sun and an array of objects that orbit it. These objects include the nine known planets, their 64 known moons, asteroids, comets, meteoroids, and huge amounts of gas and dust. The Sun's great size relative to the other objects in the solar system gives it the gravitational pull *(see page 16)* to keep them permanently in orbit around it.

The planets orbit the Sun in the same direction (counterclockwise in this illustration) and in elliptical (oval-shaped) paths. Pluto's orbit is the most elliptical of all the planets. For part of its journey around the Sun, its orbit actually lies inside that of Neptune. All the planets, and most of their moons, travel on approximately the same plane, with the exception of Mercury and, once again, Pluto, both of which have tilted orbits.

Constantly streaming away from the Sun in all directions is the solar wind, made up of electrically charged particles (parts of atoms). Traveling at more than 248 miles (400 km) per second, it produces electric currents inside a giant magnetic "bubble" called the heliosphere. The heliosphere protects the solar system from cosmic rays arriving from space. Its edge, some 11,180,000,000 miles (18 billion km) from the Sun, marks the true boundary of the solar system.

On this diagram of the solar system, the orbits of the planets are represented by colored rings. (The size of the planets and their relative distances are not to scale.) A number of unmanned spacecraft, called space probes, have been launched to explore the solar system. They include *Pioneer 10* (the first probe), *Voyagers 1* and *2*, and *Galileo*.

Voyager 1 *space probe*

Saturn

Neptune

Voyager 2 *space probe*

Nicolaus Copernicus (1473–1543)

EARLY ASTRONOMERS

Thousands of years ago, in the time of the ancient civilizations of Egypt and China, people thought that the Sun and Moon were gods, Earth was flat and the sky was a great dome suspended above it.

In later years, astronomers from ancient Greece proved that Earth was round. Many believed that the stars were fixed to a great sphere that rotated around Earth each day. One Greek astronomer, Aristarchus, proposed that the planets, including Earth, orbited the Sun, a star, but most astronomers of this time thought that the Sun, Moon, and planets all traveled in

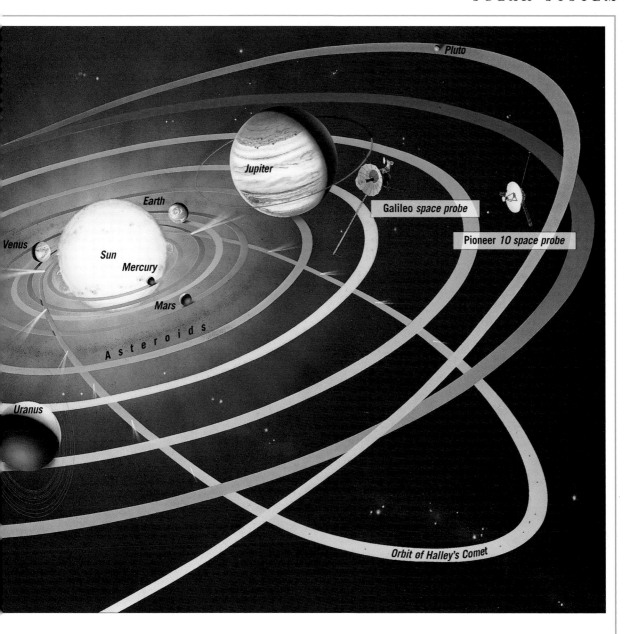

circular paths around Earth, the center of the universe. Ptolemy, who lived in the 2nd century A.D., observed that, while the stars moved across the night sky along regular paths, the planets appeared to "wander" from theirs. He proposed that they each moved in their own small circles, called epicycles, as they orbited Earth.

The Polish priest and astronomer, Nicolaus Copernicus, challenged Ptolemy's view of the solar system, declaring that the Sun lay at the center of a system of orbiting planets. Only the Moon orbited Earth. Copernicus wrongly believed that the planets' orbits were perfect circles and that

they moved in epicycles. It was left to the German astronomer Johannes Kepler (1571–1630), who showed that the planets moved in elliptical, rather than perfectly circular, orbits. The shapes of their orbits also explained the "wandering" that so perplexed earlier observers, thus disproving the idea that the planets moved in epicycles.

The Italian astronomer Galileo (1564–1642) was the first to use a telescope. From his observations of the moons of Jupiter in orbit around that planet, and the changing shape of Venus as it orbited the Sun, he concluded that Copernicus had been correct: The planets do orbit the Sun.

THE SUN

THE SUN is an ordinary star. To us on Earth it is of crucial importance since no life could exist without it, but it is simply one of billions of stars in the Milky Way Galaxy *(see page 34)*, itself one of billions of galaxies in the universe. For a star, the Sun is below average size—some astronomers classify it as a "yellow dwarf." Yet it is massive when compared to the planets. The Sun contains more than 99 percent of all the matter in the solar system. Its diameter of 869,900 miles (1,400,000 km) is more than 100 times that of Earth.

The Sun is a spinning ball of intensely hot gas made up almost entirely of hydrogen (three-quarters of its mass) and helium. It produces massive amounts of energy by "burning" about four million tons of hydrogen every second.

INTERNAL LAYERS

At the center of the Sun is the core, a region of incredible pressure (200 billion times that on Earth's surface) and intense heat—about 27 million°F (15 million°C). This is the Sun's nuclear furnace, where the energy that keeps it shining is released *(see page 21)*. Hydrogen atoms fuse together to form helium. Energy from this reaction flows out from the core through the radiative zone to the convective zone. Here, in a continuous cycle, hot gas bubbles up to the surface before sinking down to be reheated again.

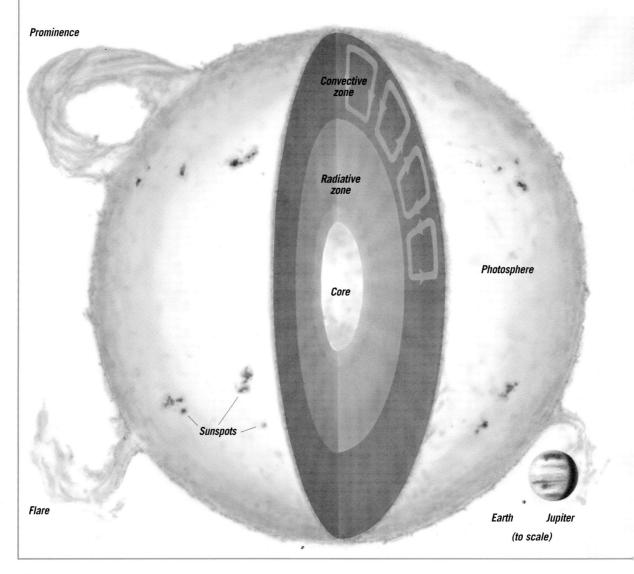

Prominence

Convective zone

Radiative zone

Core

Photosphere

Sunspots

Flare

Earth   Jupiter
(to scale)

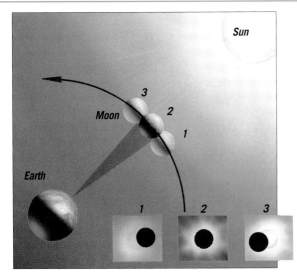

By coincidence, the Moon and Sun appear to be the same size in the sky. So when the Moon passes between Earth and the Sun *(seen in the sequence 1–3)*, it may block out our view of the Sun, a solar eclipse. During a total eclipse, an event only rarely witnessed, the Moon covers the Sun's surface entirely and the corona shines out from behind a black disc. For a short while, dusk falls. In a partial eclipse, part of the Sun still remains visible.

Invisible lines of magnetic force *(see page 31)* that twist around the Sun's globe are the cause of many extraordinary features. Huge arches of fire, called prominences, can be held up above the Sun by magnetism. Flares, sudden, massive explosions of energy, burst forth when the magnetic field shifts. Where magnetic field lines erupt through the photosphere, there are dark, cooler areas 7,772°F (about 4,300°C) known as sunspots.

Beyond the chromosphere lies the corona, the Sun's hot, shimmering outer atmosphere. This is visible from Earth only during a total solar eclipse.

In this sequence, the Sun grows to the size of a red giant.

THE SURFACE OF THE SUN

The Sun's outer shell, the photosphere, is only about 500 kilometres thick and, at 9,932°F (5,500°C), much "cooler" than at the core. It is in a state of constant motion, like water in a boiling kettle. Hundreds of thousands of flaming gas jets, called spicules, leap up to 6,214 miles (10,000 km) into the Sun's atmos-phere, known as the chromosphere.

DEATH OF THE SUN

When the Sun's fuel of hydrogen starts to run out, it will grow into a much bigger and brighter star, called a red giant. It will eventually shed its outer layers into space. All that will remain of the Sun itself will be, at first, a small, extremely dense star (a white dwarf), before it eventually cools and wastes away (a black dwarf).

About 7 billion years from now, the hydrogen that the Sun uses as fuel to create energy will start to run out. Eventually the Sun will balloon into a red giant, engulfing Mercury and perhaps Venus, too. This is what Earth's landscape may look like when this happens. Its oceans and atmosphere have gone and its rocky surface is melting in temperatures of 2,732°F (1,500°C). Venus is seen as a black dot against the Sun. It may soon be swallowed up by the colossal star.

THE PLANETS

A PLANET is a large object in orbit around a star. It can be made of rock, metal, liquid, gas, or a combination of these. Planets do not produce light, but reflect the light of their parent star.

In our own solar system, there are nine planets, including Earth, orbiting the Sun, our parent star. Observations of other stars made by astronomers using powerful telescopes indicate that they, too, have planets. There could therefore be billions of other planets in the universe.

Earth is the largest of the four inner, or "terrestrial," planets: Mercury, Venus, Earth, and Mars. They are, as the scale illustration *(below)* demonstrates, dwarfed by the four "gas giants," Jupiter, Saturn, Uranus and Neptune, so called because they have comparatively small rocky cores surrounded by thick layers of liquid and gas. Pluto fits into neither category, being a small, outer planet made of ice and rock.

The diagram at the foot of this page shows the relative distances of the planets from the Sun. Pacing out their positions would give an even better idea of the huge distances between them. If the Sun were a football, Mercury would be a pinhead 10 paces away from it. Earth (the size of a peppercorn) is a further 16 paces on from Mercury, with the Moon a thumb's length away from Earth. Another 209 paces would bring you to Jupiter (a large marble), while Pluto lies 884 more paces distant. To reach the nearest star, Proxima Centauri, you must walk another 4,163 miles (6,700 km)!

EXPLORING THE PLANETS

Because the giant planets lie so far from Earth, it would take too long for people to travel to them. So space probes have been launched to "fly by" every planet except Pluto and send back pictures. *Voyager 2 (see page 54)* made the greatest journey. Space probe *Cassini* visits Saturn in 2004.

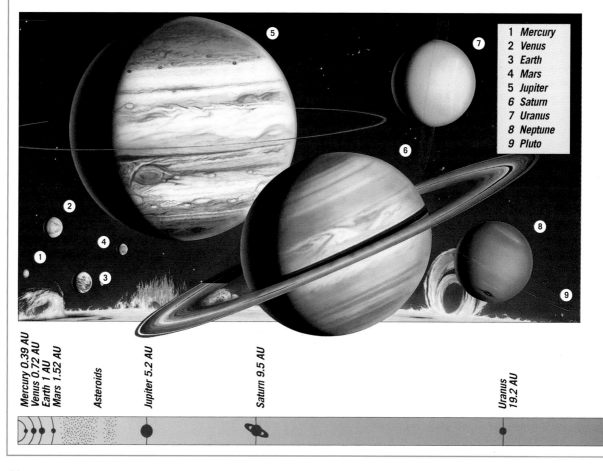

1 Mercury
2 Venus
3 Earth
4 Mars
5 Jupiter
6 Saturn
7 Uranus
8 Neptune
9 Pluto

Mercury 0.39 AU
Venus 0.72 AU
Earth 1 AU
Mars 1.52 AU

Asteroids

Jupiter 5.2 AU

Saturn 9.5 AU

Uranus 19.2 AU

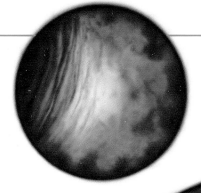

1 A shock wave, possibly from a nearby supernova, causes a cloud of gas and dust to collapse under its own gravity.

2 The collapsed cloud becomes a swirling disc of matter with a bulge at its center.

The solar wind stripped away any remaining dust and gas, including the atmospheres around the four inner planets. The giant planets lay beyond the solar wind's fiercest blast, so they were able to hold onto their thick blankets of gas.

Jupiter's gravitational pull caused nearby planetesimals to destroy one another rather than build up into another planet, leaving a belt of rock fragments, known as asteroids, still orbiting the Sun, as they do today.

3 Small fragments of rock clump together in large blocks called planetesimals.

THE PLANETS FORM

The solar system began life as a cloud of gas and dust drifting across the Milky Way Galaxy. It is thought that a supernova may have sent shock waves racing across space, striking the cloud and somehow causing it to collapse under its own gravity.

Within 100,000 years, the collapsed cloud became a swirling disc, called a solar nebula. Under pressure from gas and dust spiralling inward, the center became hotter and denser and began to bulge. It would soon evolve into the infant Sun.

Away from this central furnace, particles of dust began to clump together like snowflakes, first into small fragments of rock, then becoming large boulders. Over millions of years, some grew into blocks several miles across, called planetesimals. These eventually started to collide with one another, building up like snowballs to become the four rocky inner planets, Mercury, Venus, Earth, and Mars, and the cores of the four gas giants, Jupiter, Saturn, Uranus, and Neptune.

4 The core of the disc becomes a ball of hot gas—a star. The solar wind strips the four inner planets of their atmospheres.

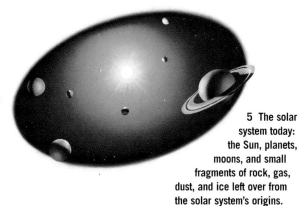

5 The solar system today: the Sun, planets, moons, and small fragments of rock, gas, dust, and ice left over from the solar system's origins.

Pluto 29.6 AU (when nearest the Sun)

Neptune 30.1 AU

This diagram *(below)* shows the relative distances of the planets from the Sun. 1 AU (Astronomical Unit) is the average distance between Earth and the Sun.

Pluto 49.3 AU

MERCURY

MERCURY, the closest planet to the Sun, is the second smallest planet in the solar system. Because it is so near the Sun, it can be seen from Earth only with difficulty—low in the dawn or twilight sky close to the Sun.

Mercury's surface looks quite similar to that of our moon. Bare and rocky, it is covered with craters, the result of continual bombardment by meteorites during the first billion years of its existence. Originally molten, Mercury's surface shrank as it cooled after the bombardment eased,

When a meteorite strikes the surface of Mercury, it punches a saucer-shaped crater in the ground. Debris is blasted out in all directions, creating long streaks.

resulting in "wrinkles"—long mountain chains. With no winds or water to erode the rocks, Mercury's landscape has remained the same ever since.

Mercury's orbit has an unusual shape All the other planets, except Pluto, have nearly circular orbits, but Mercury's is elliptical— more like an oval. At its closest, Mercury is 28.58 million miles (46 million km) from the Sun, 43.5 million miles (70 million km) away at its most distant.

Mercury has great extremes of temperature. Where it faces the Sun, it can exceed 752°F (400°C), but during the long nights (lasting about 59 Earth days) and with no atmosphere to keep the heat in, temperatures can plummet to –274°F (–170°C).

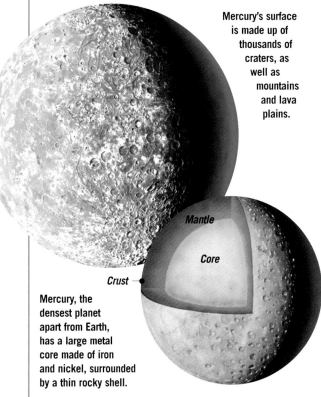

Mercury's surface is made up of thousands of craters, as well as mountains and lava plains.

Mantle

Core

Crust

Mercury, the densest planet apart from Earth, has a large metal core made of iron and nickel, surrounded by a thin rocky shell.

FACTFILE

Diameter: 3,032 miles (4880 km)
Day: 58.6 days
Year: 88 days
Average distance from the Sun: 36,040,000 miles (58 million km)
Surface temperature: -292 to +806°F (-180 to +430°C)
Atmosphere: traces of helium
Moons: none

The landscape of Mercury is dominated by thousands of craters. The huge Sun burns with a fierce heat—turning to severe cold when this face of the planet is turned away from it. Large boulders falling from space have produced craters in Mercury's surface measuring many miles across, some with smaller craters inside. Because there is hardly any atmosphere, Mercury's skies remain black even during the day.

VENUS

ABOUT THE SAME SIZE as Earth, Venus is shrouded in thick, unbroken clouds made of droplets of deadly sulphuric acid. Because its cloud cover reflects the light of the Sun from its surface, Venus is a very bright object in the night sky.

Some 15.5 miles (25 km) thick, the clouds prevent most sunlight from reaching the surface. But another kind of radiation from the Sun, called infrared, does get though and Venus's dense atmosphere stops it from escaping. The result is a constant surface

This is what Venus would look like if it were not permanently obscured by clouds. The dark areas are lava plains.

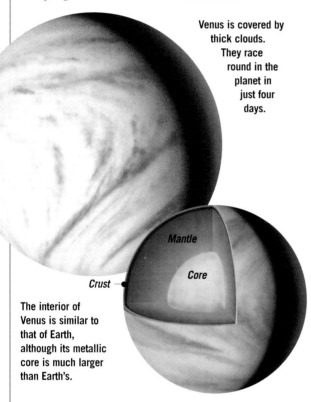

Venus is covered by thick clouds. They race round in the planet in just four days.

The interior of Venus is similar to that of Earth, although its metallic core is much larger than Earth's.

Crust — Mantle Core

temperature hotter than the melting point of lead and the hottest in the solar system. If any space explorer landed on Venus, he or she would be simultaneously incinerated, suffocated by the unbreathable carbon dioxide air, dissolved by acid and crushed by air pressure about 90 times that on Earth.

Venus spins slowly on its axis, actually taking longer to complete one rotation than to orbit the Sun. Relative to all the other planets except Pluto, it spins backwards.

FACTFILE

Diameter: 7,522 miles (12,105 km)
Day: 243 days
Year: 225 days
Average distance from the Sun: 67,110,000 (108 million km)
Surface temperature: 914°F (490°C)
Atmosphere: carbon dioxide, traces of nitrogen
Number of moons: none

Beneath the clouds, Venus's barren surface features tens of thousands of volcanoes (some possibly still active) surrounded by vast lava plains. Lava flows have cut channels in the ground that look as if they may have been carved by rivers. Odd, dome-shaped volcanoes, or "pancakes," as they have been described, have formed where lava has oozed to the surface, then cooled as it spread out in all directions.

EARTH

OUR OWN PLANET, Earth, is the largest of the four inner planets. Third in order of from the Sun, 71% of its surface is taken up by oceans. Water is also present as droplets or ice particles that make up the clouds, as vapor in the atmosphere and as ice in polar areas or on high mountains.

Liquid water is essential for the existence of life on Earth, the only body in the solar system where life is known to be present. Earth's distance from the Sun—neither too close nor too far—produces exactly the

When Earth lies directly between the Sun and the Moon it casts its shadow on the Moon. This is called a lunar eclipse.

right temperature range. The atmosphere traps enough of the Sun's energy to avoid temperature extremes. It also screens the harmful rays of the Sun and acts as a shield against bombardment by meteoroids.

Earth's magnetic field is generated by electrical currents produced by the swirling motion of the liquid inner core. The magnetic field protects Earth from the solar wind *(see page 40)*.

Earth's outer shell, made up of the rocky crust and partly molten upper mantle, is divided into about 15 separate pieces, called tectonic plates. Volcanoes and earthquakes occur where plate edges meet.

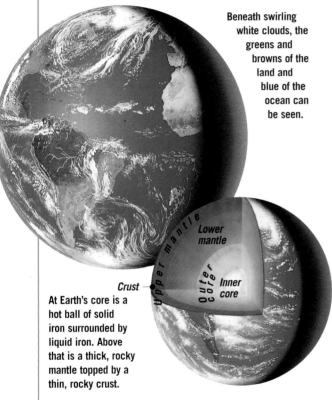

Beneath swirling white clouds, the greens and browns of the land and blue of the ocean can be seen.

Crust —
Lower mantle
Inner core
Outer core
Upper mantle

At Earth's core is a hot ball of solid iron surrounded by liquid iron. Above that is a thick, rocky mantle topped by a thin, rocky crust.

FACTFILE
Diameter: 7,926 (12,756 km)
Day: 23 hours 56 minutes
Year: 365.26 days   **Number of moons:** 1
Average distance from the Sun: 93,020,000 miles (149.7 million km)
Surface temperature: -94 to +131°F (-70 to +55°C)
Atmosphere: nitrogen, oxygen, water vapor

In contrast to the barren landscapes of the other planets, much of Earth's is covered by vegetation, including forest, scrub, and grassland. Different climates determine the types of plants and animals that live in different places. Large areas show the important influence of humans: for example, farmland, roads, and cities. Land areas are continually sculpted by the weather and moving water or ice.

MOON

THE MOON is neither a star nor a planet. It is a ball of rock that travels around Earth, taking about 27 days to complete the circle. It is the brightest object in the night sky, although the light it "shines" is reflected from the Sun.

The Moon may have formed when a large object or planetesimal *(see page 45)* collided with the newly formed Earth more than four billion years ago. The impact "splashed" into space vast amounts of debris that later came together to form the Moon.

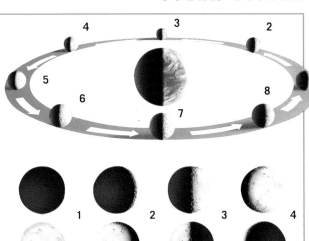

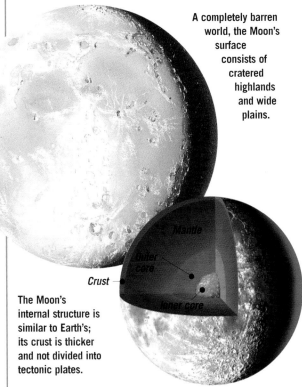

A completely barren world, the Moon's surface consists of cratered highlands and wide plains.

Mantle

Outer core

Crust

Inner core

The Moon's internal structure is similar to Earth's; its crust is thicker and not divided into tectonic plates.

PHASES OF THE MOON

The shape of the Moon appears to change from one night to the next. This happens because, as it travels around Earth *(above)*, it spins only once, so the same face remains pointed toward us at all times. It is our view of the sunlit part that changes. When the face pointed toward us is turned away from the Sun, we cannot see the Moon at all—a new moon (1). When it is turned toward the Sun, we see a complete disc—a full moon (5). In between, it passes through crescent (2), quarter (3), and gibbous (4) phases, and back again (6–8).

FACTFILE

Diameter: 2,160 miles (3,476 km)
Average distance from Earth: 239,000 miles(384,600 km)
Day: 27.3 days
Surface temperature: -247 to +221°C (-155 to +105°C)
Atmosphere: none

With neither air nor liquid water, it is impossible for plants or animals to live on the Moon. The barren lunar landscape is pitted with craters, blasted out by meteorites crashing to its surface. Scattered debris has left streaks radiating from some craters. The Moon also has wide, smooth lava plains. Early astronomers thought these were seas. They are still called by the Latin name for sea, *mare.*

MARS

ALTHOUGH Mars is much smaller than Earth, the two planets have a number of similarities. The Martian day is only a little longer than ours and its angle of tilt means that Mars has four seasons, just as we do on Earth. Daytime temperatures at the equator in midsummer can sometimes reach 77°F (25°C). Thin clouds of water vapor or early morning surface frosts can also sometimes be seen. Like Earth, Mars has volcanoes, mountains, dried-up riverbeds, canyons, deserts, and polar ice caps.

Mars's four massive volcanoes stand on the Tharsis bulge. Olympus Mons, which rises 20 km, is seen here compared to Mauna Kea, Hawaii (green summit, at far right) the tallest mountain on Earth measured from base to summit (10,205 m).

For these reasons, Mars is thought to be the only other planet where life may once have existed. However, analysis of the Martian soil by space probes *Viking 1* and *2*, which touched down on the planet in 1976, and *Pathfinder* in 1997, failed to find any sign of past or present life.

Mars is a barren planet. Its reddish color comes from iron oxide dust (similar to rust). From time to time, large dark regions appear on the surface. These are areas of bare rock, exposed when storms remove the dusty covering. The Martian landscape features some dramatic landforms. The solar system's highest mountains and its deepest canyon, Valles Marineris, are found on Mars.

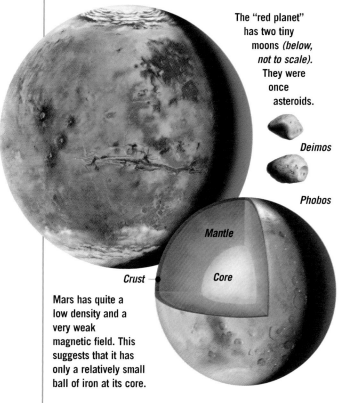

The "red planet" has two tiny moons *(below, not to scale)*. They were once asteroids.

Deimos

Phobos

Crust —

Mantle

Core

Mars has quite a low density and a very weak magnetic field. This suggests that it has only a relatively small ball of iron at its core.

A number of valleys and channels have been carved into the Martian plains. From the evidence of sediments— muds and silts deposited by water—it seems likely that there were once rivers, lakes, and even seas on Mars. The only water left on the surface today is frozen in the polar ice caps. The rest may have been lost to space due to Mars's weak gravity, or hidden from view as a deep-frozen layer beneath the surface.

FACTFILE
Diameter: 4,223 miles (6,797 km)
Day: 24.6 days
Year: 687 days
Average distance from the Sun: 141.7 million miles (228 million km)
Surface temperature: -184 to +77°F (-120 to +25°C)
Atmosphere: carbon dioxide, nitrogen
Moons: 2

JUPITER

JUPITER is the largest planet in the solar system. Large enough to contain more than 1,300 Earths inside it, Jupiter is more massive than all the other planets combined. Along with Saturn, Uranus, and Neptune, Jupiter is known as a "gas giant," because it is mostly made of gas with no solid surface at all.

The colorful patterns of red, brown, yellow, and white on Jupiter's surface are produced by the chemicals sulphur and phosphorus in the swirling atmosphere. Jupiter's extremely quick rotation is probably responsible both for separating the clouds into different color "zones" (the lighter bands) and "belts" (the darker bands), and for the continual storms. The Great Red Spot, its most famous feature, is such a storm. The quick rotation also causes Jupiter to bulge at its equator, so that it measures 4,660 miles (7,500 km) less from pole to pole.

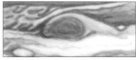
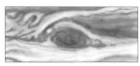
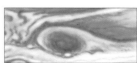

Large enough to contain two Earths, the Great Red Spot is actually a giant storm that has been raging for at least 300 years. Its topmost clouds rotate in a counterclockwise direction, taking about six days to make a complete turn. This sequence shows smaller storms (the white ovals) and turbulent air currents flowing past the spot.

Jupiter has a system of rings consisting of dark grains of dust. The four largest of its moons are bigger than the planet Pluto.

FACTFILE

Diameter: 89,410 miles (143,884 km)
Day: 9.8 hours
Year: 11.8 years
Average distance from the Sun: 483.4 million miles (778 million km)
Surface temperature: -238°F (-150°C)
Atmosphere: hydrogen, helium
Number of moons: 16

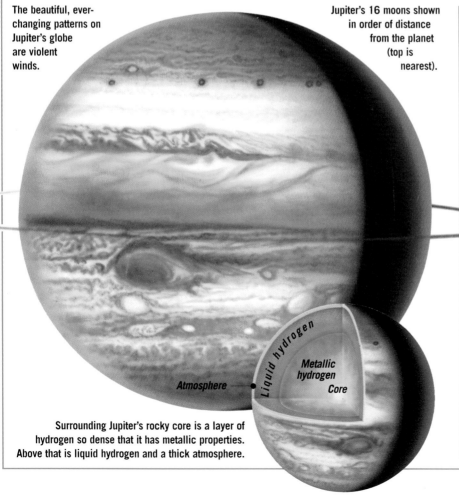

The beautiful, ever-changing patterns on Jupiter's globe are violent winds.

Atmosphere — Liquid hydrogen — Metallic hydrogen — Core

Surrounding Jupiter's rocky core is a layer of hydrogen so dense that it has metallic properties. Above that is liquid hydrogen and a thick atmosphere.

Jupiter's 16 moons shown in order of distance from the planet (top is nearest).

Metis ·
Adrastea ·
Amalthea ·
Thebe ·
Io
Europa
Ganymede
Callisto
Leda ·
Himalia ·
Lysithea ·
Elara ·
Ananke ·
Carme ·
Pasiphae ·
Sinope ·

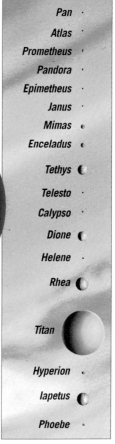

Swirling clouds and storms can sometimes be seen as ripples on Saturn's globe. Saturn rotates very quickly, producing a distinct bulge at its equator. It is the least dense of the planets: If a large enough bathtub could be found, Saturn would float in the water!

SATURN

ALL FOUR gas giants have rings, but Saturn's, visible from Earth through even a small telescope, are broad, bright, and magnificent. As detailed photographs taken by *Voyager 2* show, the rings are made up of billions of blocks of ice and rock, ranging in size from boulders as large as houses down to tiny fragments the size of snowflakes *(top right)*. They are only a few tens of metres thick. Some astronomers think that the rings are the fragmented remains of a moon that was smashed apart by a passing comet.

Three rings can be made out from Earth. The outer ring (A ring) is separated from the other two lying inside it (B and C) by a gap called the Cassini Division. *Voyager 2* spotted fainter rings beyond A ring. It also revealed that each ring was, itself, divided into thousands of ringlets.

Saturn has a large family of moons, many of which are small, irregularly shaped bodies with some even sharing the same orbits.

Saturn's 18 known moons, in order of distance from the planet (top is nearest). They are drawn to scale, relative to one another.

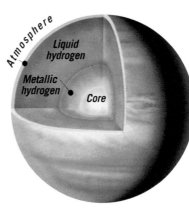

Liquid hydrogen
Metallic hydrogen
Core

Saturn's internal structure *(above)* is similar to Jupiter's.

Saturn's spinning axis is tilted so our view of its rings alters as it orbits the Sun *(below)*. At stages 1 and 7 they are invisible. At 4 and 10 they are at their widest angles.

Pan
Atlas
Prometheus
Pandora
Epimetheus
Janus
Mimas
Enceladus
Tethys
Telesto
Calypso
Dione
Helene
Rhea
Titan
Hyperion
Iapetus
Phoebe

FACTFILE

Diameter: 74,880 miles (120,514 km)
Day: 10.2 hours
Year: 29.5 years
Average distance from Sun: 886.7 million miles (1,427 million km)
Surface temperature: -292°F (-180°C)
Atmosphere: hydrogen, helium
Number of moons: 18

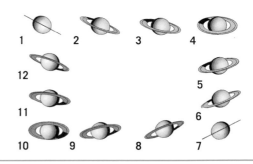
1 2 3 4
12 5
11 6
10 9 8 7

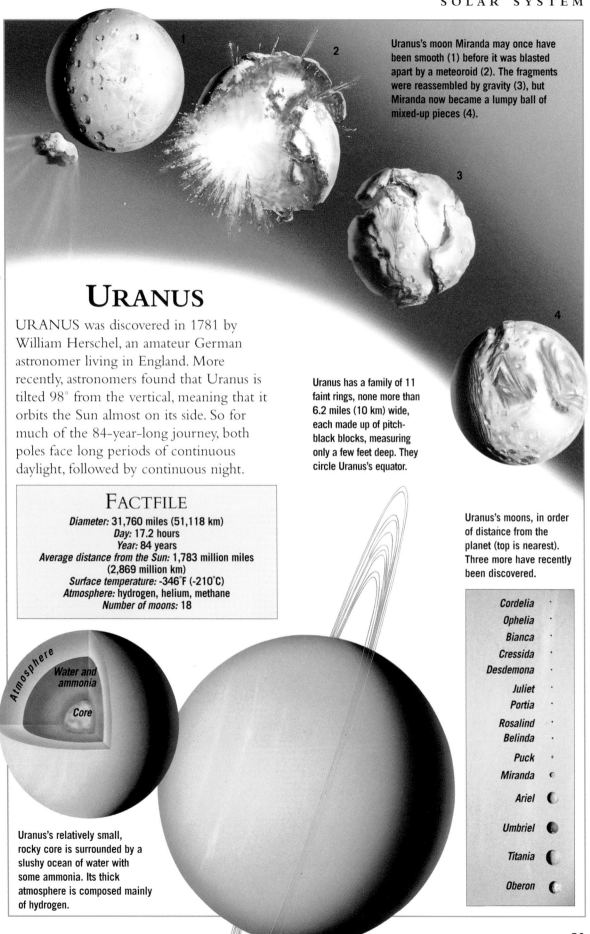

Uranus's moon Miranda may once have been smooth (1) before it was blasted apart by a meteoroid (2). The fragments were reassembled by gravity (3), but Miranda now became a lumpy ball of mixed-up pieces (4).

URANUS

URANUS was discovered in 1781 by William Herschel, an amateur German astronomer living in England. More recently, astronomers found that Uranus is tilted 98° from the vertical, meaning that it orbits the Sun almost on its side. So for much of the 84-year-long journey, both poles face long periods of continuous daylight, followed by continuous night.

Uranus has a family of 11 faint rings, none more than 6.2 miles (10 km) wide, each made up of pitch-black blocks, measuring only a few feet deep. They circle Uranus's equator.

FACTFILE

Diameter: 31,760 miles (51,118 km)
Day: 17.2 hours
Year: 84 years
Average distance from the Sun: 1,783 million miles (2,869 million km)
Surface temperature: -346°F (-210°C)
Atmosphere: hydrogen, helium, methane
Number of moons: 18

Uranus's moons, in order of distance from the planet (top is nearest). Three more have recently been discovered.

Cordelia ·
Ophelia ·
Bianca ·
Cressida ·
Desdemona ·
Juliet ·
Portia ·
Rosalind ·
Belinda ·
Puck ·
Miranda ◦
Ariel ◗
Umbriel ●
Titania ◖
Oberon ◖

Atmosphere

Water and ammonia

Core

Uranus's relatively small, rocky core is surrounded by a slushy ocean of water with some ammonia. Its thick atmosphere is composed mainly of hydrogen.

NEPTUNE

NEPTUNE was discovered by German astronomer Johann Galle in 1846. Its largest moon, Triton, was recorded a few days later. Besides that, very little was known about Neptune until the space probe *Voyager 2* visited it in 1989.

A bright blue globe, Neptune almost completely lacks surface features. At the time it was photographed by Voyager, a storm system, called the Great Dark Spot (which later disappeared), could be seen racing in a direction opposite to the planet's rotation. Winds on Neptune blow at more than 1,243 miles (2,000 km) per hour.

Like the other gas giants, Neptune has a system of rings. There are four extremely faint rings, composed of dark, icy fragments.

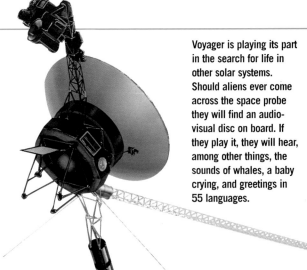

Voyager is playing its part in the search for life in other solar systems. Should aliens ever come across the space probe they will find an audio-visual disc on board. If they play it, they will hear, among other things, the sounds of whales, a baby crying, and greetings in 55 languages.

FACTFILE

Diameter: 30,790 miles (49,557 km)
Day: 16.1 days
Year: 164.8 years
Average distance from the Sun: 2,794,000,000 miles (4,496 million km)
Surface temperature: -364°F (-220°C)
Atmosphere: hydrogen, helium, methane
Moons: 8

VOYAGER 2

The greatest journey by a space probe so far undertaken was made by *Voyager 2*. Between 1979 and 1989, it flew close by Jupiter, Saturn, Uranus, and Neptune, transmitting superbly clear pictures of the planets and their moons. Voyager has since sped away from the solar system, although it continues to send back signals—20 billion times weaker than those of a watch battery!

A layer of warm water, with some ammonia and methane, surrounds Neptune's rocky core.

Neptune's blueness arises from the small amounts of methane found in its atmosphere. The white streaks are fast-moving clouds.

(Bottom) Neptune's eight moons, are shown in order of distance from the planet (top is nearest). They are drawn to scale, relative to one another.

Atmosphere

Water, ammonia and methane

Core

Naiad ·

Thalassa ·

Despina ·

Galatea ·

Larissa ·

Proteus ·

Triton

Nereid ·

PLUTO

PLUTO is the smallest, coldest, and outermost planet in the solar system. It was the last to be discovered, identified in 1930 by the American astronomer Clyde Tombaugh. He compared photographs of part of the sky taken six days apart and noticed that a pinprick of light had moved slightly against the background of stars. Pluto was the only outer planet not visited by *Voyager 2*, so astronomers still know little about it. Some even propose that Pluto is really a comet and not a planet at all.

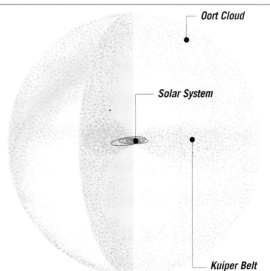

Thousands of icy objects may exist in the outer reaches of the solar system. They may form either a belt (the Kuiper Belt) or a cloud (the Oort Cloud). This could be the birthplace of comets *(see page 58).*

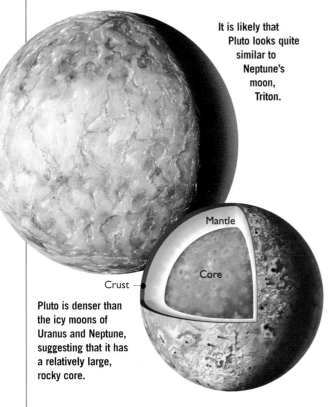

It is likely that Pluto looks quite similar to Neptune's moon, Triton.

Pluto is denser than the icy moons of Uranus and Neptune, suggesting that it has a relatively large, rocky core.

Pluto has a very elongated orbit, ranging between 7,400 and 4,400 million kilometres from the Sun, bringing it inside the orbit of Neptune for part of the journey. Pluto's moon, Charon, is just over half its size and lies only 19,640 kilometres away from it. Both spin in a direction opposite to that of the other planets except Venus.

FACTFILE

Diameter: 1,429 miles (2,300 km)
Day: 6.4 days
Year: 248 years
Average distance from the Sun: 3,675,000,000 miles (5,914 million km)
Surface temperature: -364°F (-220°C)
Atmosphere: probably nitrogen and methane
Number of moons: 1

Pluto's surface is probably an "icescape" of frozen nitrogen, carbon monoxide, and methane. There may be craters made by collisions with rock and ice fragments. Seen from Pluto, the Sun looks no more than a bright, distant star. It still provides just enough heat to evaporate some of the surface frost and create an extremely thin atmosphere. Charon, Pluto's nearby moon, features prominently in the sky.

MOONS

MOONS, also known as satellites, are relatively small worlds that orbit the planets of the solar system. Earth has one moon, known simply as the Moon *(see page 49)*, but other planets have many more—Saturn, for example, has at least 18 moons.

All seven of the moons illustrated here *(below)* are larger than the smallest planet, Pluto, while the largest moons, Ganymede and Titan, are even bigger than Mercury, the second smallest planet. Jupiter's four largest moons are all in the top seven. They are called the "Galileans" after the Italian scientist Galileo Galilei who first discovered them with one of the first telescopes in 1610. Ganymede has an icy surface with cratered plains and areas showing strange "grooved" patterns.

Titan

Callisto

Io

Ganymede

Moons are very varied in size and form. Many have unusual landscape features that intrigue astronomers.

Moons are created in different ways. Some are the result of fragments of rock or ice being pulled together by gravity to form a globe. Others are asteroids that have been "captured" by a planet's gravitational force.

Titan, Saturn's largest moon, is the only moon to have a thick atmosphere, made mainly of nitrogen. Beneath its continuous cloud layer, there may be a sea of methane.

The surface of Jupiter's moon Io may look like this. There are volcanoes everywhere. When they erupt, plumes of sulphur dioxide gas burst through from Io's rocky interior, jetting some 186.4 miles (300 km) into space. Astronomers think it is likely that Io is being affected by the enormous gravitational pull of Jupiter (and nearby moon Europa), which tugs at the moon, creating sufficient heat inside it to cause the eruptions.

The blue-green globe of Uranus, about 80,160 miles (129,000 km) away, dominates the skies of one of its moons, Miranda. The landscape of this moon, a jumble of cliffs, canyons, and craters, looks as if it has been patched together from many different landscapes *(see page 53)*. There is a distinctly V-shaped zone of "grooves." One great cliff is 12.4 miles (20 km) high, well over twice the height of Earth's highest mountain, Mount Everest.

Callisto, Jupiter's second largest moon, is heavily cratered. Measuring 372 miles (600 km) across, its most prominent crater, called Valhalla, is surrounded by a series of ripples. Io, the third of Jupiter's Galileans, with its crust a vivid mixture of yellows, oranges, reds, and blacks, looks a little like a pizza. In fact it is peppered with active volcanoes and lakes of molten rock.

Our own moon is the fifth largest moon in the solar system, although it would take 81 moons to make up a world the size of Earth. The Moon's lava plains indicate past volcanic activity, but there are no active volcanoes there today.

Next in order of size comes Europa, the fourth Galilean and an object of great interest amongst astronomers. Looking like a cracked egg, its surface consists of ice sheets that are continually melting and resolidifying. It is by no means impossible that, beneath those ice sheets, there is a warm ocean of liquid water. Could it be that life has also evolved on Europa and that there are life-forms swimming in its oceans? Future space probe missions may find out.

Triton is Neptune's largest moon. Its surface is the coldest place known in the solar system. At –391°F (–235°C), the temperature is low enough to freeze nitrogen. Triton was photographed in stunning detail by *Voyager 2*, the last of its close encounters, in 1989.

Moon

Europa

Triton

The surface of Triton, Neptune's major moon, is made up of a deep layer of mainly granite-hard nitrogen ice. Sometimes the ice melts to a slush before quickly refreezing, producing ridges and cracks. Nitrogen in its gaseous form collects beneath the solid ice crust. The pressure builds up and eventually the nitrogen gas erupts through weak points in the crust. Gas and dust are spurted up to 5 miles (8 km) high.

COMETS

COMETS are potato-shaped lumps of dust measuring only a few miles across, but accompanied by (when near the Sun) tails of gas or dust that stretch for hundreds of millions of miles across space. The lump of dust is fused together by frozen gases and water ice. Like all other objects in the solar system, comets orbit the Sun, although their orbits are often very elliptical (elongated ovals), looping in towards the Sun from distant reaches of the solar system. When a comet approaches the Sun, part of its ices melt and the gas and dust escape, forming a surrounding cloud, or coma. As it rounds the Sun, the coma is swept back into two tails, a straight gas tail and a broader, curved dust tail, always pointing away from the Sun.

Gas tail

Dust tail

A comet has two tails: a straight gas tail and a broader, curved dust tail. They grow as the comet approaches the Sun. The comet passes round the Sun. Its tails, still pointing away from the Sun, shorten and disappear as the comet retreats to the outer Solar System.

This is a view (below) of a comet's nucleus, a lump of dust frozen together. When it comes near to the Sun, the ices melt, the outer crust of the nucleus cracks open and jets of dust and gas gush out to form a cloud called a coma.

Sometimes, small pieces of debris break off from comets. Great showers of these fragments, called meteors, sometimes come quite close to Earth. Millions of tiny particles burn up in Earth's atmosphere. Commonly known as shooting stars, they appear to us as split-second streaks of light in the night sky.

On June 30, 1908 there was a huge explosion in the Tunguska region of Siberia, Russia. Trees in an area about 62 miles (100 km) across were felled by the blast, but no crater was found. The Tunguska fireball may have been a comet exploding at an altitude of about 3.7 miles (6 km).

FAMOUS COMETS

The English astronomer Edmund Halley (1656–1742) was the first to realize that comets were orbiting objects. He once made a famous prediction: A comet that he observed in 1682 would return to the skies in 1758. Halley believed that comets recorded in 1531 and 1607 were simply earlier sightings of the one he saw in 1682. Halley did not live to see his prediction come true. Halley's Comet, as it has been known ever since, was duly sighted on Christmas Day 1758 and has reappeared every 75 to 76 years. When Halley's Comet appeared in March 1986, the space probe *Giotto* flew within 372 miles (600 km) of it, sending back pictures and sampling the gases and dust particles given off by it.

A sighting of a comet is always a great event. The 1997 appearance of the Hale-Bopp Comet was the most spectacular of recent years. Comets can also be destructive if they pass too close to a planet. In July 1994, drawn in by gravity, fragments of the Shoemaker-Levy Comet smashed into Jupiter, creating massive fireballs on impact.

ASTEROIDS

ASTEROIDS are small, mostly rocky, irregular-shaped bodies. They are found orbiting the Sun in a band filling the 341.8-million-mile (550-million-km) gap between Mars and Jupiter. The largest, Ceres, measures just under 621 miles (1,000 km) across, but only a handful have diameters greater than 62 miles (100 km). About 4,000 have been recorded, but there are many thousands more too small to be identified.

Astronomers believe that, during the formation of the solar system *(see page 45)*, Jupiter's strong gravitational pull caused nearby planetesimals to smash into one another rather than build up into another planet. This left the belt of fragments we call the asteroids.

Most asteroids are rocky, indicating they come from the outer layers of a former minor planet. But some are metallic—they come from the core of such a planet.

The asteroids have continued to collide with one another since their formation, producing smaller fragments called meteoroids. These have occasionally crashed on to Earth's surface (when they are known as meteorites). It is feared that one day a large meteorite may devastate Earth, causing climatic change sufficient to wipe out many life-forms.

A close-up view of the irregular shaped objects that make up the asteroid belt between Mars and Jupiter. From study of asteroid fragments that have fallen to Earth, scientists have dated the age of the solar system at 4.6 million years.

GLOSSARY

Acid A reactive chemical. Strong acids are corrosive—they can break down and dissolve substances easily. Strictly, an acid is a substance capable of donating hydrogen ions for chemical reaction.

Alkali Like an acid, a reactive chemical. It is a base dissolved in water.

Asteroid A rocky body that orbits the Sun. Asteroids range in size from tiny specks to about 1,000 km in diameter. They are sometimes known as minor planets.

Atmosphere The envelope of gases surrounding a planet, moon or star.

Atom A basic building block of matter. It consists of a nucleus, made up of protons and neutrons, surrounded by a number of electrons.

Base A compound that reacts with an acid to form a chemical salt.

Big bang The origin of the universe, which took place in a gigantic explosion from an incredibly hot and dense state about 15 billion years ago.

Black hole A region of space from which nothing, not even light, can escape. Its force of gravity is much more powerful than any normal star in the universe.

Chemical reaction The process by which the chemical properties of a substance are changed, or a new substance formed.

Comet An object made of dust and ice that orbits the Sun, usually following a very elongated oval path. On nearing the Sun, it develops a cloud of dust and gas (a coma) and two very long tails.

Compound A molecule that consists of atoms of more than one element, for example, water, a compound of hydrogen and oxygen.

Conduction The flow of energy through a substance. It occurs as the molecules inside the substance vibrate, transferring their vibrations from one molecule to the next.

Constellation A group of stars forming a pattern in the sky.

Convection current The movement of heat through liquids and gases. Heated from below, a liquid or gas will expand, become less dense, and rise. Away from the source of heat, the opposite will occur, and the liquid or gas will fall.

Crater A saucer-shaped feature found on the surface of many moons and asteroids, and some planets. It is formed by the impact of meteorites.

Crystal A solid substance with a regular geometric shape, including naturally formed flat sides at certain angles to each other.

Density A measure of how compact something is. An object is denser than another if its atoms are larger or more tightly packed together.

Eclipse The passage of one planet or moon in front of another, totally or partially obscuring it from an observer. In a solar eclipse, the Moon passes between the Sun and Earth, blocking out the Sun's light.

Electromagnetic spectrum The complete range of electromagnetic radiation, the form in which certain kinds of energy, such as radio, infrared, light, ultraviolet, and X rays, are transmitted through space or matter.

Electron A subatomic particle that orbits the nucleus of an atom. The electron carries a negative electrical charge, while the protons in the nucleus are positively charged. Positive and negative charges attract each other, so the atom is held together.

Element A substance composed of atoms of the same type that cannot be broken down by chemical means into simpler substances. Lead, hydrogen, and carbon are all elements. All matter in the universe is made up of 92 natural elements.

Energy The ability of something to do work, make an event happen, exert a force, or cause change in some way.

Force Something that changes the movement or shape of an object.

Friction A force that resists (acts against) the movement of one surface against another.

Galaxy An enormous collection of stars, gas, dust and planets. Galaxies are gathered together in clusters.

Gravity The force that attracts all objects to each other. The larger an object's mass (the amount of matter it contains), the greater its gravitational pull. The greater the distance between objects, the smaller the force of gravity between them.

Ion An atom that has become electrically charged by the loss or gain of electrons. One that has lost electrons is positively charged, while one that has gained them is negatively charged.

Magnetic field The region surrounding a magnet, an object which has two ends, called poles, and a force of attraction between them.

Magnetism The invisible force of attraction or repulsion between materials, especially those made of iron.

Mass A measure of the amount of matter in an object.

Meteorite A meteoroid that falls from space to land on the surface of a planet or a moon.

Meteoroid A small lump of rock that hurtles across the solar system. Many meteoroids were once parts of asteroids.

Molecule The smallest part of a substance that can exist by itself and still possess its chemical properties. A molecule consists of atoms, either of the same type or a combination of different types bonded together.

Moon A smaller object that orbits a planet, also known as a natural satellite.

Nebula A cloud of gas or dust in space.

Orbit The circular or elliptical (oval-shaped) path followed by one object round another. For example, the Moon orbits Earth, while Earth orbits the Sun.

Planet A smaller object that orbits a star. Planets do not radiate their own light, but reflect the light from the star.

Pressure The amount of force acting on a certain area.

Quasar The center of a very violent galaxy.

Radiation The transmission of heat, light and other forms of energy through space.

Radioactivity Particles or rays given off by unstable atoms, for example, uranium.

Solar system The solar system consists of the Sun, together with the planets, their moons, comets, asteroids, meteoroids, and a mass of gas and dust that circle round it.

Solar wind A stream of subatomic particles flowing away from the Sun.

Space probe An unmanned spacecraft guided from Earth. Some have, for example, passed close by, or landed on the surface of other planets and moons.

Star A globe of gas that produces heat from nuclear reactions inside its core and radiates energy from its hot surface.

Subatomic particles Constituent parts of an atom. They include electrons and the protons and neutrons found in the atomic nucleus.

Supernova The massive explosion of a supergiant star.

Universe Everything that exists—all matter and space.

Weight The force an object possesses when the gravitational force of another object acts upon it.